# Thomas Hardy's ENGLAND

# Thomas Hardy's ENGLAND

Introduced and edited by
**JOHN FOWLES**
written by
**Jo Draper**

LITTLE, BROWN AND COMPANY
BOSTON    TORONTO

Conceived and produced by Pilot Productions Limited, 59 Charlotte Street, London W1P 1LA, England

First published in the United States in 1984 by Little, Brown and Company (Inc.), 34 Beacon Street, Boston, Massachusetts 02106, U.S.A.
Published simultaneously in Canada by Little, Brown & Company (Canada) Limited

Photographs (except those mentioned below) Copyright © 1984 by James and Gregory Stevens Cox
Photographs on pages  8, 28, 44, 46, 53, 56, 57, 63, 64, 65, 67, 68, 72, 73, 90, 91, 92, 95, 96, 105, 108, 112, 115, 127, 130, 131, 133, 136, 137r, 139l, 143, 144 top r, 146, 147, 157, 168, 172, 177r, 178r, 179, 180, 184, 185 reproduced by kind permission of The Dorset Natural History and Archaeological Society, Dorset County Museum, Dorchester, Dorset, England.
Photograph on page 132
reproduced by kind permission of the Lyme Regis Museum, Lyme Regis, Dorset, England.
The photograph on page 24 appears by courtesy of MGM/UA Entertainment Company
Extracts from letters by Thomas Hardy reproduced by permission of the Thomas Hardy Estate

Library of Congress Catalog Card Number 84–81113
FIRST AMERICAN EDITION

Typesetting by Dorchester Typesetting Limited, Trinity Street, Dorchester, Dorset, England
Origination by Clan Studios Limited, Clan Works, 1 Howard Road, Bromley, Kent BR1 3QJ, England
Printed by Printer industria grafica s.a., Saint Vicenç dels Horts, Barcelona, Spain
D.L.B. 27447-1984

# CONTENTS

## Acknowledgments

James and Gregory Stevens Cox own the copyright in the photographs taken by Hermann Lea and George and Harold Baker, and in many by Richard Hine. Their photographic collection and longtime interest in Thomas Hardy originally inspired the production of this book.

James Stevens Cox has devoted his life to historical, literary and archaeological pursuits. He was a Member of the Council of the Somerset Archaeological Society from 1949 until 1967 and Honorary Editor of the Proceedings of the Dorset Natural History and Archaeological Society between 1955 and 1976, when he became the Society's Vice-President. He is the editor of seventy-two monographs on the life, times and works of Thomas Hardy, the co-editor of *The Thomas Hardy Yearbook*, and the author of *The History of Ilchester*, for which work he was elected a Fellow of the Society of Antiquaries.

Gregory is co-editor and publisher of *The Thomas Hardy Yearbook*, the author of numerous pamphlets on local history, classical studies, Thomas Hardy and related topics. At the age of sixteen he was awarded a place at Oxford University and subsequently won an Open Exhibition. He graduated in both Classics and Oriental Languages (Arabic with Turkish), and received his M.A. in 1972. Like his father, James, he lives on the island of Guernsey, where besides his writing and publishing activities, he is Classics master at Blanchelande College.

## Author's acknowledgments

I am very grateful to John Fowles for asking me to collaborate with him. I thank him for all his encouragement and opitulation, and for his having improved my text. We are both particularly grateful to Joe Bettey and Michael Millgate for reading the typescript and for their comments. I owe much to Meriel Ensom, Mr and Mrs T. W. Jesty, Dr Sadie Ward and Nigel Webb for information about the photographs and other matters. I have made extensive use of Joe Bettey's *Rural Life in Wessex 1500–1900* (1977), Michael Millgate's *Thomas Hardy, A Biography* (1982), and Sadie Ward's *Seasons of Change – Rural Life in Victorian England* (1982).

Sheena Pearce has kindly typed successive versions of the manuscript with speed and skill. I also thank the staff of the Reference Library, Dorchester, for their patience. I am indebted to Roger Peers and Christopher Chaplin for reading the text, and for all their help during the production of the manuscript. Finally, my greatest debt is to my parents, whose knowledge of farming and rural life has helped me so much.

J.D.

# Introduction by John Fowles

A purist might perhaps complain that the title of this book of photographs is not strictly accurate. In many respects, not least in popular imagination, Thomas Hardy's England is the England of his young manhood (he was born in 1840), well before the period when most of the pictures here were taken. One might say it was even earlier still, since he never forgot, and often used, many of the stories his mother and grandmother had told him. By the middle of his life he himself was very well and sadly aware that the ancient and immemorial Dorset of his early years was changing deeply in countless social and economic ways. Quite apart from the evidence in his novels and poems, he wrote one of the shrewdest sociological accounts of its passing. The figures and ways of life we see here were often, at the time of taking, already becoming picturesque relics rather than the living or common reality. Nor of course are we truly dealing with England, but with the fluid-boundaried part of it, as much imaginative as geographical, that Hardy called after the Dark Age kingdom of the West Saxons: Wessex.

If Hardy's Wessex is to include every geographical scene in his works, we have to cover a considerable area. To the east it reaches at least to a line drawn south from Oxford to Winchester, and to London beyond; to the west, to the Scilly Isles in Cornwall; it must include the modern counties of Berkshire, Wiltshire, Hampshire, as well as the true South West of Somerset, Dorset, Devon and Cornwall. But any map of this diffuse 'theatre' (as Hardy called it) soon shows, by the frequency of the thinly disguised fictional names he gave to real places, where its core lies. It is much

*Thomas Hardy with his bicycle, and Emma Hardy with her nephew; outside Max Gate, about 1900. Probably taken by the Reverend Thomas Perkins, since his tricycle is just visible, background left.*

smaller; not even all of Dorset, but overwhelmingly the East and North of it, and above all the area close to where he was born, and grew up. Bockhampton lies only three miles from the centre of Dorchester, the county town. Between 1862 and 1881 he was often living away from this heartland. But then he spent all the last half of his life, from 1885 to 1928, at Max Gate (so called from a turnpike gate-keeper named Mack), which is even closer to Dorchester, and still only just over two miles from his birthplace. An extraordinary number of places famous in both his work and his biography – Puddletown, Stinsford, Kingston Maurward, 'Egdon Heath' – lie within a radius of a few miles.

We tend, naturally enough before the size and breadth of his work in literary and human terms, to think rather too largely of Hardy in biographical ones. That jealously preserved and frequently concealed Dorset peasant self that lies somewhere near the heart of so much of his creation springs essentially from a very small landscape. It is easy enough now to denigrate the sometimes rather snobbish doublings he went in for in his later years to escape the hounds of his own humble past; just as it is to sneer at his self-designed house at Max Gate. There is, I think, no greater shock in English literary biography than to go round that far from distinguished villa just outside Dorchester, set on its rather bleak upland. It neither matches that environment, which he has made so vivid in words, nor any conception of Hardy gained from his books; and can conform rather painfully to almost every prejudice we may have against Late Victorian taste and the middle-class ethos behind it.

To stand inside Max Gate, and remember what came out of it – *Tess of the D'Urbervilles*, *Jude the Obscure*, *The Dynasts*, the countless poems . . . that is when most of us feel we should give up trying to understand great writers. We come expecting the palace of a maker of a fabulous kingdom; and are faced with a brick mediocrity, more suitable to a successful local merchant of his time than anything else. But to put it so ignores the huge distance that Hardy had come, both economically and socially, from his beginnings. He may well have felt

Max Gate was a leap enough in a world where everyone knew his real past. Harold Voss, the professional chauffeur who used to drive Hardy on his tours in later years, recalled that Hardy's father and his own grandfather were both small builders, and sometimes worked together. As a small boy Hardy often had to take messages between the two (six miles, to Dorchester and back), and would get threepenny tips. It was the great writer himself who told Voss this one day; his snobbish side was never simple.

At any rate my collaborator, Jo Draper, and I hope that this book will help resolve the paradox a little, for all the scenes it shows would have been intensely familiar to Hardy's eyes, and represent, far better than Max Gate, the raw material from which he built his novels and poems. Indeed, as you will learn, many of them (or their close equivalents) were lovingly described by him in words. I suspect we may think of Max

Gate as the kind of neutral matrix where his masterly power of close and particular recall functioned best; a much more fertile environment for the writer than any of the romantic and history-drenched old Dorset houses the more conventional of his readers might expect him to have settled on, and in, for the latter and 'famous' half of his life.

Hardy has long been regarded as a valuable source for local history. In this he is rivalled only by his older contemporary, the poet-philologist William Barnes (1801-1886). Dorset remained, all through Barnes' life and so well into Hardy's, something of a national byword for its backwardness and the infamous conditions in which a large part of its agricultural poor lived. The fact that one of the key events in British trade union history, the Tolpuddle Martyrdom of 1834, took place in Dorset (and only five miles from Hardy's birthplace) was no coincidence. The county has been fortunate in terms of orthodox history, since John Hutchins's *History and Antiquities of the County of Dorset*, first published in 1774, is one of the best – if not the best – of that kind ever written in Britain. But it has very little to say, even in later editions, about the indigenous poor and their culture. Barnes worked particularly on their rich native dialect, in a version of which he wrote most of his poems; while Hardy wove into his fiction not only a great deal of native custom and folklore, but also (obeying that important function of his art that records society) gave us many pictures of what rural Dorset was like in his youth, and even earlier. Hardy himself was fully aware of this historical function. He wrote in the general introduction of 1912 to the Wessex Edition of the novels: 'Yet I have instituted inquiries to correct tricks of memory, and striven against temptations to exaggerate, in order to preserve for my own satisfaction a fairly true record of a vanishing life.'

Hardy knew the old Dorset for the very simple reason that he was of it, and very much *not* as most of us must be today, quasi-tourists, visitors from outer space, however sympathetic and nostalgic we may feel before his writing, or that of Barnes. He did rather pretend as he grew older that he took a more or less scholarly, antiquarian view of it himself; but a private emotion keeps slipping through, and is quite naked in much of his poetry and fiction. History chose to begin to destroy the old rural world very soon after he was born into it, and part of his general pessimism and determinism must be closely associated with that process.

*Hardy's birthplace, Upper Bockhampton; about 1890.*

When Edmund Gosse asked his celebrated question – 'What has Providence done to Mr Hardy that he should rise up in the arable land of Wessex and shake his fist at his Creator?' – at least one answer Hardy could have given was that the culture he was born into at the Bockhampton cottage – that of his mason father and servant mother – had been destroyed. Never mind that his acute shyness, his increasing fame, the need to placate his unmistakably (but normally, for the time) snobbish first wife, and other intellectual and artistic factors all led him to dissociate himself outwardly from his real past and family circumstances; public dissociation is not suppression. The child remains father to the man. The photographer Hermann Lea's niece, Joyce Scudamore, made some shrewd comments on Hardy when she came, as a friend of his second wife during the First World War, to know the forbidding old man. She said he was 'wrapped in himself and his writing'. She did not like his novels, finding them morbid and

*Thomas Hardy, taken by Lea, probably 1900s.*

immoral, and thought them due to 'some terrible early experiences'. And she wrote this: 'For an imaginative writer, he showed little imagination in life for some of the living. His relationships did not appear to me to be like those of other men. It was as if there hung a veil between him and the present.'

Most serious writers would, I think, recognize this syndrome and its underlying cause: an inability to bury the past, and not least because it seems more the present than the present itself. Hardy's dilemma was that his literary and social success – in the context of the rigid Victorian class-system – inexorably turned him into an outward or seeming denier of his own past; yet inwardly he remained vitally dependent on it. If he had remained only an architect (Hardy's first profession), he might have severed all connection, and taken Max Gate and all it stood for as reasonable ambition reasonably fulfilled. But writers cannot cut the umbilical cord so easily; they have to lead split lives – authentic and inauthentic ones, in the later vocabulary of existentialism. Yet the deep sense of loss this self-exile engenders, the guilt, the sense of the wasteful futility of human history, is a very valuable thing for a writer, since it is also a deep source of energy in creation. All novelists are in a sense undertakers or morticians, concerned to give the past a decent, or at least a thorough, burial. We are all reporters at a wake of that kind.

I think myself that Hardy's astounding and continuing popularity all over the world, even compared with other great novelists, can be at least partly explained by the fact that his central loss, or wake, was of an ancestral culture. It is not just the woman Tess who dies, but a whole manner of life; and it is not enough to say (remembering its hardness, its flagrant exploitations and injustices) good riddance. Something of its poetries and moods, its humour and simplicity, its courage and innocence, always remains to be mourned . . . and even envied. At first sight it may seem bizarre that Hardy should be so respected in Japan, for instance; but only at first sight. He matches perfectly a trait in the Japanese soul, a travail and loss they too have passed through, and on whose debit and credit balance they cannot decide.

Much depends, in this latter, on whether we think of the past in moral or aesthetic terms. Like Barnes a little earlier, Hardy has left us a rich and unforgettable image of a lost world. He judged himself that a new one was determined, had to come, and that it was best for most that it should. But whether that old utilitarian standard truly repaid the loss elsewhere for him, we may doubt. An equally perceptive writer across the Atlantic, Thoreau, complained two decades before Hardy of one of the great practical causes of the loss, the railway. He speaks of the increased obsession with money, the greed it has brought to the New England countryside. 'This is one of the taxes which we pay for having a railroad. All our improvements, so called, tend to convert the country into the town. But I do not see clearly that these successive losses are ever quite made up to us.'

Rather oddly the historians have not settled on any name for the huge metamorphosis that took place in British rural society during the second half of the nineteenth century. Perhaps this is because its manifestations are too vast, its causes likewise, and its progress too long drawn-out, to be easily comprehended as a single event; nor of course was it, except spasmodically and indirectly, ever a political revolution, with a clear climax. It was never planned, it merely happened. But the bare statistics of rural depopulation reveal the hugeness. Four-fifths of the nation were village or very small town dwellers in 1801; half the nation had moved to the cities and large towns by 1851; and three-quarters, by 1901. The nearly one million agricultural labourers in 1851 were cut by a third fifty years later; and today, I am told, there are more hairdressers in Britain than farmwokers.

To a striking degree it was a predominantly cultural upheaval, a profound change, over a century long (though most intense between 1870 and 1914), in the way the countryside lived. It has sometimes been described as a technical and agricultural revolution – the transition from the old labour-intensive system (which in many ways had altered very little from that of medieval and manorial England) to the final and grim destination of the mechanized and monoculture farming, or agribusiness, of our own times; but that seems to me to limit its real effect far too much. It is less that a hundred old agricultural and rural everyday crafts, from hedge-laying and coppicing to hay-making and carthorse-handling, were slowly extinguished, or survive now only as rare special skills. A complete tradition of surviving in rural conditions, not only a whole manner of life, but an unconscious philosophy of it, also disappeared.

The victims here were less human beings than their ways of working and behaving, of seeing and being. Nothing withstood the Great Change – not folk-song (though the last of the Dorset kind were mercifully recorded by the Hammond brothers in 1905-7) or folk-speech; not clothes, domestic habits or superstitions; neither family nor community relationships. To be sure many aspects of the old country life have been artificially resurrected, in matters as far apart as fabric design and thatching; while a very bastard image of its supposed virtues (ludicrously ignoring the contemporary reality of the factory farm and the universal need in farmers nowadays to pursue high-production rather than quality) remains in constant use – or misuse – in advertising. But all these siren-calls of the 'country-fresh' and the 'traditional' are transparently commercial, and largely repeat the Victorian urban myth of rural England, that comfortable vision maintained in art by sentimentalists such as Birket Foster; even when old-fashioned methods and recipes and 'natural' products are used in the home, one may usually safely guess that it is a middle-class one, and driven at least in part by a mixture of *chic* and nostalgia.

We must risk that last sin in this book. It is very difficult to present the old rural past without creating this nostalgia, precisely because nowadays we have the bastard versions of it thrown so continually at us: that is, the implication that the old countryside must have been more beautiful, more peaceful, more worthy, more stable and reliable – all that our present world is not. But Hardy is right: very few of the victims of the Great Change can have finally regretted it. They may sometimes have hated it where it hurt most directly – in the loss of jobs caused by first the steam and then the internal combustion engine, the new labour-saving machinery, and so on; but behind many of the picturesque photographs here there lies, as Jo Draper often points out in her accompanying text, a very unpicturesque and generally bitter story of unrewarded and

Jude-like lives. The rural masses were undoubtedly culturally impoverished by the Great Change; but if that had to be the price of escaping from the more literal and far more terrible impoverishment of most labouring and living conditions, who is to deny it – and who  seeing the price we still pay, not to regret it also?

Hardy wrote one of his finest non-fiction pieces for the July number of *Longman's Magazine* in 1883. It was called *The Dorsetshire Labourer*, and is a very valuable corrective to our stock notions of the farm labourer, or at least to our notion of his existence as one of the monotonous misery. Hardy suggests with a convincing sarcasm that 'Dick the carter, Bob the shepherd, and Sam the ploughman are, it is true, alike in the narrowness of their means' . . . but they emphatically cannot be rolled together into one uniform type, the 'Hodge' of middle-class mythology. He adds that 'drudgery in the fields results at worst in a mood of painless passivity'; while at least the field labourer has 'a pure atmosphere and a pastoral environment' by birthright. He is equally sceptical about dirt as a chief proof, to the well-educated (and very often socially – rather than genuinely – pious) Victorian outsider, of ingrained misery and low morale. 'Melancholy among the rural poor arises primarily from a sense of incertitude and precariousness of their position.'

The precariousness arose very largely from the annual hiring-fair system, whereby the farmer bought his labour for each next year. In 1883 Hardy recalled that it was much changed even in his lifetime; now the hiring was based on a written agreement (as opposed to the old handshake and shilling handsel), and already there was a significant change in clothes – the old smock had begun to disappear, along with the traditional symbols of particular trades. Many labourers now wore their Sunday best to such fairs. The great day was the old Lady Day (April 6th), for that was when the agreements had to be honoured, and the roads were crowded with labourers and their families moving to new cottages on fresh farms. 'It is not possible to walk a mile of any of the high roads this day without meeting several.' Only a generation before, continues Hardy, not one cottage on a farm changed hands yearly; but 'Dorset labourers now look upon an annual removal as the most natural thing in the world.'

This restlessness meant labourers had by the 1880s become a good deal less simple than before. 'They are losing their peculiarities as a class.' Being constantly shuffled, like a pack of cards, also meant that they had become far less locally attached in their feelings. 'They vent less often the result of their own observations than what they have heard to be the current ideas of smart chaps in towns'; and Hardy says the women have often gained the 'rollicking air' of factory hands. This was Thoreau's 'railroad tax'. The country was not only being magnetized to the towns and to foreign countries such as America and Australia, from both of which attractive reports must frequently have percolated back; but the spirit of the town was invading the countryside. Hardy comes to the nub of it in the following passage.

'That seclusion and immutability, which was so bad for their pockets, was an unrivalled fosterer of their personal charm in the eyes of those whose experiences had been less limited. But the artistic merit of their old condition is scarcely a reason why they should have continued in it when other communities were marching on so vigorously towards uniformity and mental equality. It is only the old story that progress and picturesqueness do not harmonise. They are losing their individuality, but they are widening the range of their ideas, and gaining in freedom. It is too much to expect them to remain stagnant and old-fashioned for the pleasure of romantic spectators.'

The result was of course a painful (and ever-growing) dissociation of man from land, and also of the farmer from his men, now that they were valued strictly according to their labour-worth, rather than for their past knowledge of 'fields . . . ploughed and known since boyhood'. The children were not the least to suffer in this breaking of the old ties with familiar life-time place and master. Hardy reported, of one village school he knew in that same year of 1883, that well over a third of the previous year's pupils had disappeared on Lady Day – forced to follow their parents to new work and new places.

Wages in 1883 had risen in general to some eleven or twelve shillings a week (fifty-five or sixty pence in modern currency, although inflation makes comparisons misleading) from the seven or eight of earlier in the century. There were generally extra sums for special work, called tut-work, such as harvesting and haymaking, besides various customary perquisites, such as the cheap rent (two pounds per annum at Corfe in the 1840s) for cottage and garden, right to a quarter-acre of potato ground, and some wood for burning. Extra sums could also be earned by the labourer's wife and children – turnip-hoeing like Tess, stone-picking and bird-scaring – but these were occasional and even more miserably paid than the men. Every such family hoped for sons rather than daughters.

Pregnancy before marriage was a very common custom, indeed almost universal in remoter communities; and was widely interpreted as wicked immorality by the more respectable. There were several cases of this in Hardy's own family, and he himself, an eldest child, was conceived three months 'before the altar'. A report in 1846 mentions the especially unfair position of unmarried men, who were paid even less, at five or six shillings a week, yet expected to work as hard. Their crime was not providing more hands for the future, and this was why ensuring the future bride was fertile was much less wickedness than a wise precaution. But the state of farm cottages was often atrocious, a matter aggravated by this economic pressure to overbreed; add to that the general penury, and it is no wonder that child mortality was high.

Many girls had to go away into service, and thus became – if we may believe that other great witness to Victorian rural England, Flora Thompson in *Lark Rise to Candleford* – important if unconscious agents in the Great Change. They returned back home with a host of new ideas absorbed from their jobs and mistresses, very often in the latter's cast-off clothes; and for the first time let their more sedentary parents and brothers know the meaning of culture shock. Flora Thompson tells a story that epitomizes it. Such a young bride, returned home from service to marry and faced with a first visit from her new in-laws, put a vase of sweet peas on the meal-table. Her labouring father-in-law regarded them with extreme puzzlement. 'Danged if I ever heard of eatin' they before,' he said.

Hardy ends *The Dorsetshire Labourer* by saying that all these changes by no means came uniquely from 'agricultural unrest'. Another important rural class, the one he had himself been born into, that of the small tradesman or craftsman, and shopkeeper, who effectively owned their own small houses or cottages on a lifehold lease (they were called 'liviers'), was being driven away to the towns, not least because the all-powerful local land-owners wanted all available property for their farm labourers, and had no time for this 'unattached' element in their villages. This was before mechanization bit; but of course even when it did, the reduced work-force simply meant fewer customers.

The immensity and final destination of the Great Change is still not easy for us to grasp today, and it must have been far more difficult at the time. Hardy himself, only four years after *The Dorsetshire Labourer*, was sounding a less humane and sympathetic note. He wrote that he was 'equally opposed to aristocratic privilege and democratic privilege. (By the latter I mean the arrogant assumption that the only labour is hand-labour – a worse arrogance than that of the aristocrat . . .)' He was even more positive in 1891. 'Democratic government may be justice to man, but it will probably merge in proletarian, and when these people are our masters it will lead to more of this contempt [for non-manual work] and possibly be the utter ruin of art and literature.' This is clearly the new middle-class owner of Max Gate speaking, as also the writer now taken up by the aristocracy (and finding them much more conversable than he had in some of his earliest novels). Hardy was never really a political person; yet he remained to the end of his days a Liberal in practical terms, and a liberal in the more modern sense.

One final irony will be well-known to anyone who has, as I have, tape-recorded stories of old people born in the 1880s and 1890s: the immense difficulty of

*A child and scarecrow in the strawberry bed at Bardolf Manor, near Puddletown, taken by Lea about 1895.*

persuading them, even on their own often abundant evidence, that they were not happier then. That they somehow were seems an almost universal feeling among those who recall the lost world of before 1900, or even 1914. I have just been reading a collection of such memories recorded in Appalachia, in the United States. Childhood after childhood of appalling deprivations and poverty; yet hardly a person who does not recall it with a warmth, love and affection very seldom shown for all the outward improvements in life since. One may subtract as much as one likes for the notorious golden distortion of memory; yet there is still something, a secret, that none of our politicians or sociologists seems quite to have penetrated. Perhaps it is made of those losses Thoreau spoke of, that are never quite made up to us.

We know very little of what Hardy himself felt about photography. One may suspect he had divided feelings. He would certainly have been attracted by its physical power of recall; but it is difficult to believe that he – especially Hardy the poet – can have liked its intrinsic dangers as a mere substitute eye. He speaks disparagingly several times of the photograph in words, 'that inartistic species of literary produce', and applies it to the slice-of-life novel, for which he had little sympathy. At a time when some postcards were based on his novels, he laid down these guidelines: 'All I stipulate is that each picture shall be pleasing and romantic in itself, and that no view shall be used, however truthful in fact, which is bald and prosaic as a picture.'

We often forget that Hardy also went through the experience that faces all modern best-sellers – seeing his work adapted to the screen. *Tess of the D'Urbervilles* was filmed in 1913 by Adolph Zukor's Famous Players company; and again by Metro-Goldwyn in 1924. *Far from the Madding Crowd* was shot in 1915, *The Mayor of Casterbridge* in 1921. Hardy met the actors and crew for this last production outside the famous Dorchester inn, the King's Arms, and was surprised that the worthy townspeople showed no interest whatever in the spectacle, despite the actors' yellow make-up and antique clothes. Of *Tess* in 1913 he specified in negotiations that 'it must not be vulgarized or treated lightly, so that all possibility of a farcical view of the tragedy is prevented'; and warned that he would not stand for a happy ending being substituted. On October 21st that year he was in London and saw what sounds like a rough cut (he rather mysteriously calls it 'a rehearsal or review') of the film. 'It was a curious production, & I was interested in it as a scientific toy; but I can say nothing as to its relation to, or rendering of, the story.'

An extract from a 1920 interview with Vere H. Collins is also revealing.

*C. There are some very pretty photographs in Hermann Lea's book* (Thomas Hardy's Wessex, *1913*).

*H. Yes. He never intended to write a book at first, but after taking all the photographs he thought it was a pity not to put them to some use. I fear he has not made any money out of it. That is a pity. It discourages a man from going on writing.*

Collins said he was amused at Lea's caution in identifying real with fictional places. He always employed some qualifying phrase.

*H. That is the result of my coaching. I impressed on him that no place is taken exactly from an existing one.*

Hardy knew, of course, like every other writer, that no fiction can be literally tied to any one choice of real places, that it must always spring from a combination of them – and that some places will have no literal counterpart at all. 'Some are undoubtedly composite structures', Lea himself admitted in his introduction to *Thomas Hardy's Wessex*; and he added later that there is 'a tendency to confuse the ideal with the actual'. (His own 240 photogaphs in the book are certainly more ideal than real, since respect for Hardy seems to have made him favour the orthodox, unpeopled and often distinctly dull 'postcard' view, in photographic terms. We reproduce only a very few of these here; they are not truly typical of his work and quite certainly not of his lively real character.)

Lea was an engagingly unusual man. He did not meet Hardy in the flesh until 1898, though he had long been an admirer of his work. The two men seem to have hit it off from the start; the reserve, or mask, that Hardy showed so many other male admirers and visitors was soon conquered. It may have been partly because Hardy knew by 1898 that he had given up the novel, and Lea's idea of systematically photographing their real-life sites helped keep them alive in his mind. At any rate he showed himself remarkably willing to act as Lea's adviser and companion when he went photographing, and a considerable liking and understanding grew between the two men. It was confirmed in 1913, when Lea moved into Hardy's birthplace, the cottage at Bockhampton, and with the great man's full approval.

Lea had been born in 1869 in Essex (his mother was German), but then came as a young man, in 1888, to study farming at a well-known Dorset country house,

*Hermann Lea's Irish Terrier.*

Athelhampton, near Puddletown, some six miles east of Dorchester; in other words, in the heart of Thomas Hardy's closest and most native landscape. He later moved nearer Dorchester, into a house partly designed by himself. He was a skilled gardener and bee-keeper, a keen cyclist, a vegetarian, and must have been one of the first to put up bird nesting-boxes. Like Hardy he was a determined enemy of vivisection and all cruelty to animals (at one period he carried this last belief so far that he would not even wear leather shoes). He was bearded, as Hardy had once been; and rather short, as Hardy also. He also had a formidable will, balanced by a strong sense of humour, which again matched Hardy's own temperament very well.

His nephew, Alfred Scudamore, recalls travelling by train with Lea to London; at every stop Lea stood at the carriage window and behaved 'in a peculiar manner' – in fact grimacing and gesturing like an unmistakable lunatic. They duly kept the compartment to themselves. He was eccentric in dress, as well; and was immensely proud (before nicotine truth emerged) of an Irish terrier he had taught to smoke. 'Uncle was one of the great Dorset characters, and those who knew him best will remember him for his generosity, independence of thought, strong compassion, unconventional habits, complete indifference to popular opinion, a strong streak of Rabelaisian humour and a great strength of will. He would sometimes take offence easily.'

Lea was also an early car-owner, though he never lost his love of the bicycle. He owned first a tiller-steered Oldsmobile, then by 1901 he had a Hupmobile. Lea had been interested in photography long before the 1898 meeting, and indeed that was brought about through

The Reverend Thomas Perkins, vicar of Turnworth 1893-1907. He was a friend of Hardy, and took many photographs illustrating the novels, some of which are used in this book. This photograph was probably taken at Turnworth Hardy could have pressed the button. Perkins was a vegetarian, and supported the Anti-Vivisection League.

*Hermann Lea's camera mounted on bicycle wheels, probably for towing behind his bike.*

the agency of the Rector of Turnworth, the Rev. Thomas Perkins, secretary of the Dorset Photographic Club, and himself a friend of Hardy. Perkins was also an antiquary, and shared in the campaign on behalf of animals. He died in 1907. Both Lea and Perkins had already photographed many sites from the Wessex novels, and they wanted to produce an illustrated edition of them. This proved not possible, and so they fixed on the idea of sets of relevant postcards. It was to discuss this that the three men met.

Hardy soon took an active part in the project, which was successfully carried out, and subsequent ones, and frequently joined the many excursions on foot, or by bicycle and car. He was, in Lea's own words, 'exceedingly helpful in identifying some of the less obvious spots', though always careful to stress the difference between the fictional imagination and the camera plate. When Lea proposed *Thomas Hardy's Wessex*, Hardy did not seem very interested at the beginning, but warmed to the idea as it progressed. His close friendship with Lea continued after publication by Macmillan in 1913. Lea recorded 36 car tours with Hardy in 1915; and 32 in 1916, when petrol was rationed; in that last year he also paid 54 visits to Max Gate.

Lea was no Boswell. He did write some sketches for a biography of Hardy, with many interesting minor anecdotes and accounts of their days together, but also a distinct reserve whenever Hardy unbound and talked of his personal past. Lea felt these 'confidences' could in no circumstances be divulged, and they went with him to the grave. Literary researchers may curse him here; but I think most novelists would do the very reverse. Despite the two men's differences of age and background – and talent – it is clear they were in many things fellow-spirits. The lively biographical sketches show us a rather different older Hardy than is commonly presented – certainly a more outgoing, and humorous, one.

Lea told him how one lady whose permission he sought to photograph a house was not impressed. 'Lor', we're just pestered with people coming here every since that book were wrote – I wish the man had hanged hisself afore he got it finished.' 'That book' was *Tess of the D'Urbervilles*, and Hardy was much amused. Another lady was even more direct. 'Why could not he have done some building like his father, instead of writing a lot of rubbish that no one wants to read?' Living as he did at Bockhampton, Lea was well aware of the price of Hardy's fame, and had some sharp meetings with would-be intruders. Hardy's gardener recalled having to repel 'charabanc loads' of unwanted visitors at Max Gate; according to Hardy's doctor 'American visitors' were often to be seen 'hanging round his gate'. Some even knelt there.

Lea left Bockhampton in 1921, seven years before Hardy's death, and for the next three decades lived some thirty-five miles away at Linwood, in the New Forest, Hampshire. He died in 1952, just three days short of his eight-third birthday. Some of his photos went to the Dorset County Museum, but a very considerable part were acquired from Mrs Hermann Lea by the Dorset bookseller and antiquarian, Mr J. Stevens Cox, who now lives in Guernsey. Many of these have never been made public before, and show a much more interesting and lively side of his work than the rather formal photographs in *Thomas Hardy's Wessex*. Some of them are amusingly transparent 'fakes' in a purely historical sense: that is, obviously posed, with

*Hermann Lea's camera being demonstrated outside Bardolf Manor about 1895. It appears to be home-made; the upper tube was probably a view-finder, while the lower took the picture. The camera was capable of quite fast exposures in bright light, but interiors would have been a problem.*

people dressed to 'look past', or as Hardy characters, rather than in their normal clothes. They were perhaps done when a photographically illustrated edition of the novels was first mooted.

To these have been added a number of photographs from a collection made by Richard Hine of Beaminster (1860-1939). Hine was a chemist, but gathered together many old photographs of his native town, of which he also wrote a history. Mr Stevens Cox has also kindly allowed us to choose some photographs from another collection in his possession. Here we cheat a little, for the photographer, George Baker, evidently worked as often outside as within Wessex; we believe mainly in Shropshire and Herefordshire. Unfortunately neither Mr Stevens Cox nor ourselves have been able to discover anything about him, but he was clearly one of those prescient men who knew what historians of the future would want to see in terms of the street scene and small-town life. Finally we have included hitherto unseen photographs from the massive Dorset County Museum collection. These include some by that distinguished photographer known as Anon, to whom all historical record is permanently in debt.

I must now pass the writing into the excellent hands of Jo Draper, whose knowledge both of Hardy's texts and of the county past far exceeds mine. Her experience as the editor of the annual Dorset Natural History and Archaeological Society *Proceedings*, and her familiarity with all the sources and resources of county scholarship, to say nothing of her own rural Wessex background, make her eminently well suited to the task of commenting on this lost world and its most famous celebrant.

John Fowles, 1984

# Hardy's England

Our house stood quite alone, and those tall firs
And beeches were not planted. Snakes and efts
Swarmed in the summer days, and nightly bats
Would fly about our bedrooms. Heathcroppers
Lived on the hills, and were our only friends;
So wild it was when first we settled here.

Thus Hardy recorded his grandmother talking about the cottage where he was born in 1840, in his earliest surviving poem, written before he was twenty-one. His great-grandfather had built the house in 1801 for his grandparents in the valley of Upper Bockhampton three miles east of Dorchester, in a wild uncultivated area of woodlands and heath. By the time Hardy was a child the wild ponies (heathcroppers) had gone, but newts (efts) and snakes were still common. His mother once found the infant Hardy asleep in his cradle, inside the cottage, curled up with a large snake.

Hardy lived in the tiny hamlet of Upper Bockhampton† until he moved to London in 1862. He described it as 'a world of shepherds and ploughmen . . . where modern improvements were still regarded as wonders'*. He returned to his birthplace in 1867, and apart from short periods living in London or Weymouth, lived there with his parents until 1874. He wrote all or part of his first five novels there, including *Under the Greenwood Tree* (1872), which is set in Bockhampton and nearby Stinsford, and *Far from the Madding Crowd* (1874). He felt that it was 'a great advantage to be actually among the people described at the time of describing them', Bockhampton 'being within a walk of the district in which the incidents are supposed to occur'.

Hardy married Emma Gifford in 1874, and was only a visitor to the cottage thereafter. His family lived there until 1912, and the next year Hermann Lea, who took many of the photographs in this book, moved in.

†Also known as Higher Bockhampton both in the nineteenth century and today.
*Some of the many quotations from Hardy's work do not indicate every omission.

*Hardy's birthplace with the heath behind.*

Hardy's father was a small builder, while his mother had been a cook and house-maid. Many of his relatives were relatively poor. Hardy later tried to represent his origins as middle class, which they certainly were not. So much of his fiction deals realistically and sympathetically with the lives of agricultural labourers and craftsmen, that today we are delighted to share in his first-hand experience of their lives in his own humble beginnings. But Hardy was too much a victim of Victorian social snobbery to accept that himself.

Hardy went to school in the county town of Dorchester, and later worked in an architect's office there. After their marriage the Hardys lived in Sturminster Newton (Dorset), Upper Tooting (South London), and then at the small town of Wimborne in East Dorset, finally returning to Dorchester in 1883, and building themselves a house – Max Gate – on the outskirts of the town by 1885. Hardy had worked as an architect until 1872 and designed the house himself. His father and his brother Henry built it, and here Hardy lived for forty-three years, until his death in 1928: Thus he lived at Dorchester or Bockhampton for seventy-two of his eighty-seven years. Although he disguised his origins he can hardly have wanted to escape them: Dorchester was the one place where both his origins and social aspirations were known by everyone.

He continued writing fiction after moving to Max Gate: his last novels *Jude the Obscure* and *The Well-Beloved* were published in 1895 and 1897. In 1898 his first volume of poetry – *Wessex Poems* – was published. Such a well-known novelist turning to verse caused surprise, and it was some time before he was fully accepted as a poet. Many regretted that he had given up writing fiction, but others had found *Jude* well beyond the pale of respectability, and were glad that that side of his life was done with. Between 1898 and his death Hardy published eight volumes of poetry and *The Dynasts*, an epic drama in verse.

His first wife Emma died at Max Gate in 1912, when she was seventy-two. In 1914 Hardy, then seventy-four, married Florence Dugdale, aged thirty-five. Hardy died in 1928: she survived him and lived at Max Gate until her death in 1937.

# HARDY'S ENGLAND

The map shows the area described in the book, as it was in 1900 when Hermann Lea took many of his pictures.

Shaftesbury

YEOVIL    Sherborne

BLACKMOOR VALE

Sturminster Newton

Crewkerne

Okeford Fitzpaine

Durweston

Ibberton    Blandford

Woolland    Turnworth

Stoke Wake

London and South Western Railway (Yeovil & Exeter Br.)

Great Western Railway

Evershot

Cerne Abbas

RIVER STOUR

Beaminster

Mapperton

Maiden Newton

Wimborne Minster

Dorchester & Southampton Br.

Wooton Fitzpaine

Waterston    Bere Regis    Bloxworth

Piddletown    Woodbury

Tolpuddle

Lyme Regis    Bridport

Stratton

RIVER PIDDLE

BOURNEMOUTH

Eype    Winterbourne Abbas    DORCHESTER    Woodsford    Poole

Burton Bradstock    Winterbourne Steepleton    Came    Whitcombe    London and South Western Railway (Dorchester & Southampton Br.)

Maiden Castle    Wool    Wareham

Monkton    Warmwell    RIVER FROME

Abbotsbury    Owre Moyne

RIDGEWAY    PURBECK HILLS

Ringstead    West Lulworth    Corfe Castle

WEYMOUTH BAY    Lulworth Cove    Swanage

WEYMOUTH

CHESIL

Portland Isle

Bill of Portland

N

MILES    5    10    20

36

# Village Life

Puddletown, three miles east of Bockhampton, was the village Hardy knew best as a boy. He had many relatives there, including some of his mother's brothers and sisters. Puddletown (then still known by its proper name, Piddletown, after the River Piddle) would have rejected the designation 'village' – with 1,334 inhabitants in 1859 it probably considered itself a small town. *The Post Office Directory* for that year gives some idea of the inhabitants: 11 people are listed as 'Private Residents', that is the upper classes and the clergy, and there is a much longer 'Commercial' list, including 12 farmers, 2 dairymen, a corn merchant, someone described as builder, blacksmith and wheelwright, 2 other blacksmiths, a plumber, 3 stonemasons (one Hardy's uncle, Christopher Hand), a miller, and a man who was a currier, leather seller, rope manufacturer, saddler and harness maker. The more domestic suppliers included 7 shopkeepers, 3 bakers, 2 butchers, a grocer, 2 tailors, 2 dressmakers (including Hardy's cousin, Rebecca Sparks) a milliner and dressmaker, a watch and clock maker, a glove and gaiter maker, and 6 boot and shoe makers, one of whom was Hardy's uncle John Antell. A surgeon, and a man who combined being a herbalist and dentist, looked after the population. Two school-mistresses – one for the National School, the other for the infants – instructed the children. Communication was by a carrier who went to Dorchester every Wednesday and Saturday, and by the mail cart, which delivered letters to the Post Office every morning at 8.00 a.m.

In his introduction to *Far from the Madding Crowd* (set at Puddletown) Hardy says that the village was at one time 'notoriously prone' to drinking. The *Directory* lists two inns and two beer houses, but does not list Warren's Malthouse or its equivalent, where so much cider was drunk in the novel. The bulk of the population is omitted from the *Directory* – the labourers and servants.

As a child and young man Hardy frequently visited Puddletown, especially to see his mother's sisters. Maria, the oldest sister, had married James Sparks, a cabinet maker not listed in the 1859 *Directory*, and Mary married John Antell, a shoe-maker on whom Jude is said to be partly based. Elizabeth Hardy, the widow of one

*The centre of Puddletown in 1891. Hardy knew Puddletown before it was tidied up by a reforming landowner, who bought the estate in 1861 and spent the rest of the nineteenth century rebuilding the village in a rather heavy gothic style. The centre of the village was not altered very much by the new building.*

of Hardy's great-uncles, also lived in Puddletown and was visited by the young Hardy. He had many cousins there – his two aunts had ten children between them.

Puddletown must have formed a great contrast to Bockhampton and Stinsford, where Hardy actually lived. In the same 1859 *Directory* there were only 5 farmers, 2 dairymen, 2 shopkeepers, a shoe-maker, and a man who combined being a blacksmith and a beer retailer, for the whole of Stinsford, Bockhampton and two other hamlets. If Puddletown was almost a small town, Stinsford was hardly a village.

The people of Bockhampton, Stinsford and Puddletown were all part of the very isolated, undeveloped, rural countryside of Dorset, and had their own distinct dialect and customs, traditions and

*Hardy's mother's cousin, Stephen Burden, making an announcement to a few of the inhabitants of Puddletown, in the 1880s or 1890s. Town and village criers kept a busy and practical function, and were not merely picturesque, well up to the First World War.*

superstitions. Hardy enjoyed hearing the tales of the past and local events that his older relatives, especially his mother and grandmother, told. He recalled his grandmother in 'One we knew'.

> She showed us the spot where the maypole was yearly planted
>     And where the bandsmen stood
> When breeched and kerchiefed partners whirled, and panted
>     To choose each other for good . . .
>
> With cap-framed face and long gaze into the embers
>     We seated round her knees
> She would dwell on such dead themes, not as one who
>                                                 remembers,
>         But as one who sees.

Hardy was born just in time to catch the tail-end of the isolated old world of Dorset, and to record it in many of his novels. In the general introduction to the Wessex novels he wrote, 'At the dates represented in the various narrations things were like that in Wessex: the inhabitants lived in certain ways, engaged in certain occupations, kept alive certain customs, just as they are shown doing'. Hardy thereby hoped to 'preserve for my own satisfaction a fairly true record of a vanishing life':

'In comparison with cities, Weatherbury [Puddletown] was immutable. The citizen's *Then* is the rustic's *Now*. In London twenty or thirty years ago are old times; in Paris ten years; in Weatherbury three or four score years were included in the mere present, and nothing less than a century set a mark on its face or tone . . . In these Wessex nooks the busy outsider's ancient times are only old; his old times are still new; his present is futurity' (*Far from the Madding Crowd*).

The traditional life of the village was particularly disturbed by the increased mobility brought about by the railways. Hardy wrote in the introduction to *Far from the Madding Crowd* that mobility had 'led to a break of continuity in local history, more fatal than any other thing to the preservation of legend, folklore, close inter-social relations, and eccentric individualities. For these the indispensable conditions of existence are attachment to the soil of one particular spot by generation after generation.'

In the same novel we see some of the labourers of 'Weatherbury'/ Puddletown as Bathsheba pays them. Joseph Poorgrass does 'carting things all year, and in seed time I shoots the rooks and sparrows, and helps at pig-killings'; all this for less than ten shillings (fifty pence) a week. Besides many male labourers like him Bathsheba employs two women – Soberness and Temperance – who work 'tending thrashing machines, and wimbling haybonds [trussing hay], and saying "Hoosh" to the cocks and hens when they go upon your seeds, and planting Early Flourballs and Thompson's Wonderfuls with a dibble [potato-planter]'. These are the inhabitants of Puddletown that the directories ignore.

The picturesque thatched cottages of the villages and hamlets contained large families trying to live on very small incomes. Hardy does not lump all the inhabitants together as 'cottagers' or, in nineteenth-century terminology, 'Hodge'. He knew their lives, and the great variations found under similar roofs. His 1883

*This shop in Puddletown, about 1890, looks a little larger than those Hardy described in* The Dorsetshire Labourer, *'whose stock-in-trade consisted of a couple of loaves, a pound of candles, a bottle of brandy-balls and lumps of delight, three or four scrubbing brushes, and a frying pan'.*

article *The Dorsetshire Labourer* tried to remove the idea that 'Hodge is a degraded being of uncouth manner and aspect, stolid understanding, and snail-like movement,' and suggested that experience of life amongst rustics would show that there was as much variety among agricultural labourers as among any other body of people.

In some of the cottages there was only just enough food and shelter to support life, and in bad times not even that. As a young man Hardy knew a shepherd boy who died of starvation, an autopsy revealing that his stomach contained only raw turnip. In the late 1840s the terrible conditions of the Dorset labourers were discussed in letters and articles in *The Times*, and in 1846 the

41

*Illustrated London News* published an article on 'The Peasantry of Dorset' which showed that in one of the villages visited, Stourpaine, 'bread formed the principal, and I believe the only kind of food which falls to the labourer's lot'. The village was filthy: 'A stream, composed of the matter which constantly escapes from pigsties and other receptacles of filth, meanders down each street, being here and there collected into standing pools, which lie festering and rotting in the sun . . . the worst malignant fevers have raged here at different times . . . The wages here in very few instances exceed seven shillings per week.'

Hardy does not include the very poorest prominently in his novels, although his characters are always aware of the threat of pauperism, and the workhouse. Fear of this last deeply haunted the Victorian poor, both rural and urban. Before 1834 each village had dealt with its own poor in small poor-houses, or by small cash payments, but after that date the Poor Law Unions were set up. Groups of parishes joined together to build one big workhouse centrally. This meant that villagers who could not support themselves, through illness, old age, lunacy, pregnancy outside marriage, or simply unemployment, had to leave their village altogether for the nearest Union workhouse. In 1838, these were described as 'poverty prisons'. To prevent anyone entering them except out of dire necessity, they were made as unattractive as possible. In *Far from the Madding Crowd* Fanny Robin is reduced to struggling to reach the Dorchester Workhouse in the last stage of her pregnancy, and dies there. Inmates wore a uniform, and men and women were kept in separate wings. Hardy's poem 'The Curate's Kindness' shows an old man on his way to the workhouse.

> I thought: 'Well, I've come to the Union . . .
>     The workhouse at last –
> After honest work all the week, and Communion
>     O'Zundays, these fifty years past . . .
>
> 'Life there will be better than t'other,
>     For peace is assured.
> *The men in one wing and their wives in another*
>     Is strictly the rule of the Board.'

But he finds no peace at all in the workhouse, because the kind curate has persuaded the Board to let him and his wife stay together. From 1885 old couples were officially allowed to do this.

*Unfortunately this pair of portraits taken by Lea has no identification. They were probably a married couple from Puddletown, and seem to be 'homely workfolk'.*

The provision of old age pensions from 1908 at last helped old people to survive outside the workhouse. Taken over by the local councils in 1929, many workhouses were then closed or turned into hospitals.

There were attempts by the labourers to get their lot improved: Hardy remembered his father talking about the agricultural riots of 1830 when ricks were burnt and the newly introduced threshing machines broken up. In Hardy's short story *A Withered Arm* a boy is hanged for simply being present when a rick was fired. The rioting labourers were asking for a wage of ten shillings a week and better conditions. Bere Regis, ten miles east of Bockhampton, was one of the centres of disaffection in Dorset, and Puddletown was another. The riots only lasted a fortnight before they were suppressed by the militia and the local magistrates, and the rioters punished with great ferocity.

In 1834, six labourers from Tolpuddle, five miles east of Bockhampton, were transported to Australia for trying to set up an agricultural union. Since unions were not in themselves illegal, they were tried on the grounds of having administered an illegal oath. At the end of their trial in Dorchester their leader George Loveless presented the judge with a paper which said 'My lord, if we have violated any law, it was not done intentionally; we have injured no man's reputation, character, person, or property: we were uniting together to preserve ourselves, our wives and children from utter degradation and starvation.' Hardy was later accused of making his Wessex rustics too eloquent, but George Loveless here rivals any of them. The labourers had been trying to get their wretched wages of seven shillings a week raised to ten, the average in the rest of the country. After they had been transported their wives and children were refused parish relief, but other unions came to their aid and supported them.

In 1846 the Reverend Sidney Godolphin Osborne wrote in *The Times* that 'the poor of these counties are sheltered with no more regard . . . nay, with less regard, to decency than farm beasts; they are paid wages that keep them in a condition of scarcely intermittent pauperism; their village greens and common rights are fast being taken from them [and] they are being deprived of the right of gleaning in the fields.'

There was an unsuccessful attempt to start an agricultural union in the 1860s. Then Joseph Arch started a new union in

February 1872, and by the end of the year he had nearly 100,000 members. Hardy heard him speak and wrote in *The Dorsetshire Labourer* that 'Nobody who saw and heard Mr Arch in his early tours through Dorsetshire will ever forget him . . . a man by no means carried away by an idea beyond the bounds of common sense.' From 1874 the farmers tried to destroy the union by sacking and evicting members, or by locking them out. By 1889, they had succeeded. Hardy writing some six years before that date thought that the union had succeeded in increasing wages by three shillings a week, which 'seems small; but the increase is considerable when we remember that it is three shillings on eight or nine – *i.e.* between thirty and forty per cent. And the reflection is forced upon everyone . . . that if a farmer can afford to pay thirty per cent more wages in times of agricultural depression than he paid in times of agricultural prosperity, and yet live, and keep a carriage, while the landlord still thrives on the reduced rent which has resulted, the labourer must have been greatly wronged in those prosperous times.'

In 1906 the present agricultural union was set up, but by that time many labourers and their families had left the land, either for the towns or for a new country. Only small numbers of people emigrated before about 1840 but in the period 1841-50 (and from a national population of sixteen million) over a million and a half went; about two-thirds of them to the United States of America, a quarter to Canada and the others to Australia, South America and elsewhere. Between 1851 and 1860 over two million emigrated, more than a million to the United States, and almost half a million to Australia. The peak period was 1881-90 with over two and a half million emigrants; two-thirds of these were from England and Wales, one-third from Scotland and Ireland. These figures are for the whole of Great Britain and Ireland, but we know that Dorset contributed to the totals. The population of Puddletown fell from its peak of 1,334 in 1851 to its lowest – 934 – in 1901, despite a high birth-rate. Obviously diseases took their toll, but many people must have joined the drift to the towns or a new country. In the 1870s the local paper, the *Dorset County Chronicle*, was advertising free or assisted passages to Australia and New Zealand for 'agricultural, railway and other labourers and gardeners not exceeding 35 years of age' and 'single female domestic servants'.

*A labourer returning from work. His long sideboards are traditional in Dorset. He has long gaiters over his trousers to keep them dry, the nineteenth century equivalent of rubber boots.*

*Lea's original caption on the back of this photograph is 'An unsophisticated lot': despite large families like this the Dorset countryside was falling in population during the nineteenth century. Infant and child mortality was high.*

When the 1851 Census was published a footnote commented that 'the decrease of population in Okeford Fitzpaine, Stoke Wake, Woolland, and Ibberton is attributed to Emigration'. While the population was generally rising, these Dorset parishes and a few others in West Dorset had lost up to a fifth of their population. Stoke Wake had dropped from 156 people at the 1841 census to 124 at that of 1851. Some of Hardy's relatives were amongst those who went; for example, his aunt and her family emigrated to Canada in about 1851. Thirty years later two of his Sparks cousins went to Australia.

45

The hearth inside a cottage at Ivy Down, Puddletown, in 1899. The cooking arrangements are basically medieval. The iron door of the oven can be seen in the left of the fireplace; the long spade-like implement is a peel, for removing loaves or other food from the oven, and the long spike beside it for manoeuvring the fuel in the oven. The fuel itself can be seen to the left – furze and brambles. The huge lidded iron pots are for cooking over the open hearth, suspended from the pot-hook, while the three-legged trivets beside the fire were to support smaller pots. The hinged box to the left of the fireplace was for salt, kept dry by the heat of the fire. The wooden steps on the left of the photograph, below the spade, must have been to make someone tall enough to reach something.

Pre-marital pregnancy was almost universal in the villages. In 1849 the Reverend S. G. Osborne said 'that for the most part of the ceremony of marriage is not thought of until grounds exist for the preparation of baby linen. I always think Portland is unfairly dealt with in this matter; what is said to be an ancient custom there is at least a very general habit in the rest of the country.' The custom survived later in Portland than elsewhere, and shocked visitors.

Even among the better-off villagers, as those Hardy shows, domestic life was as arduous as the work in the fields. Much of the equipment for washing or cooking was unchanged from the medieval period.

In order to cook apple pies for his party Giles Winterborne in *The Woodlanders* has to heat his oven 'tossing in thorn-sprays, and stirring about the blazing mass with a long-handled, three-pronged Beelzebub kind of fork'. These ovens were built within the thickness of the wall, like a cupboard, circular with a domed roof. Furze or bundles of small branches (faggots) were burnt inside,

*Although this was doubtless posed by Lea in the 1890s, and reminds one of Cinderella (especially the single deliberate-looking tear in her dress), the hearth and the rest of the interior is real enough. The pretty cast-iron range was a great advance, with its two ovens either side of the fire on an open hearth, although compared to modern stoves they required careful management to get the right heat at the required time.*

*There may be an oven on the right of this hearth – the photograph is not clear. The ratchet pot-hanger over the hearth was adjustable so that pots or kettles could be hung at different heights. Taken by Lea about 1908.*

directly on the floor of the oven, quickly heating the whole. The ashes were raked out, the floor cleaned, and the food placed in the oven to be cooked by the heat as it was slowly released from the oven's floor and walls. Usually bread was cooked first, as it needs a high temperature, then pastry or cakes, and finally stews. Professional bakers often cooked food for poorer people in their ovens as they cooled, for a small fee.

Many cottages had an oven on one side of the large fireplace, others had a separate bakehouse, and some had to use the open fire for all cooking. A variety of stands, hangers and cooking pots had evolved to make all types of cooking possible in the hearth, but it was a great advance when cast-iron ranges were introduced, in the early nineteenth century. These still had an open fire, but now usually burned coal rather than wood; there was at least one fully enclosed oven to the side of the fire, and often a metal plate or grill over the fire to make boiling and frying easier, and some even provided hot water. As Hermann Lea's photographs show many cottagers were still using the open hearth even into the twentieth century. They could not afford to fit ranges.

*Washing up outside a cottage, probably not Dorset, 1880s. With small cottages and large families, many household tasks were done outdoors in the summer.*

No cottage had piped water, and the occupiers were lucky if they had a well or pump close by. Many had to carry all the water they used from the village pump, or from a stream, and often the supplies were horribly contaminated, due to poor sanitation. Washing was a heavy job therefore, and made worse by the white pinafores and thick underclothes which everybody (apart from the more pragmatic gypsies) wore. Tess returns from the club-walking to find her mother 'amid the group of children . . . hanging over the Monday washing-tub, which had now, as always, lingered on to the end of the week'. Not really surprisingly, with six children besides Tess and a husband, to wash for.

The general lack of hot water (except by boiling it on the open fire), and the dust and soot made by the fire, and by lamps or candles used for lighting, made housework a lot harder. 'Nothing is more common than for some philanthropic lady to burst in upon a family, be struck by the apparent squalor of the scene and think it a frightful example of the misery of the labouring classes . . . I am credibly informed that the conclusion is nearly always based on *colour*. A cottage in which the walls, the furniture, and the dress of the inmates reflects the brighter rays of the solar spectrum is read by these amiable visitors as a clean, happy home; while one whose prevailing hue happens to be dingy russet, or quaint old leather tint, or mud colour, is thought to be necessarily the abode of filth and Giant Despair.'

Hardy contrasts two women in *The Dorsetshire Labourer*. One whose 'bedroom floors could have been scraped with as much advantage as a pigeon-loft' but who 'shone as pattern of neatness' because, as she said, ' "I always kip a white apron behind the door to slip on when gentlefolk knock, for if so be they see a white apron they think ye be clane".' The other painted her cottage burnt umber colour, and 'her dress and that of the children were mostly of faded snuff-colour, her natural thrift inducing her to cut-up a quantity of old stuffs that had been her mother's.' She had floors of 'Mayne brick – a material which has the complexion of gravy mottled with cinders. Notwithstanding that the bedlinen and underclothes of this family were like driven snow, and that the insides of her cooking utensils were like concave mirrors, she was used with great effect as the frightful example of slovenliness.' Hardy also thought that 'the grimiest families are not the poorest': that cottage freeholders were the worst.

*Fetching water from the spring at Stoke Abbott in about 1900.*

50

*Returning from the allotment, perhaps, or taking a gift of vegetables to a friend. The man's peaked cap suggests that he had been a sea-farer of some sort – he does not dress like a labourer.*

The middle- and upper-class visitors to labourers' cottages were applying their standards of cleanliness often to very overcrowded buildings. The Royal Commission on the Employment of Women and Children in Agriculture (1868) gives examples of some of the worst overcrowding. At Corfe Castle there was a family of eight living in an outhouse built for a calf, and at the 1861 Census one cottage on the heath was divided into three and housed thirty-five people. This was exceptional, but figures in the report for all the cottages in two large parts of Dorset (the Wimborne and Cerne Union areas) showed that sixteen per cent of the cottages had only one bedroom, and that a third of these contained families with more than three children. Of the 2,000 cottages surveyed only 320 had three bedrooms, so that the commonest cottage had two bedrooms for whatever size of family.

Many farmers allowed labourers land on which to grow potatoes, or for an allotment. They charged the labourers rent, or paid them smaller wages in consideration of the land. In 1868 a not very imaginative doctor thought that 'the cultivation of his little plot affords him [the labourer] recreation when his day's work is done, whereby he is kept from injurious associations and drunken habits'. Tess finds that while she has been away her family have 'eaten all the seed potatoes – that last lapse of the improvident'. She manages to obtain some more, and works on the allotment. 'The plot of ground was in a high, dry, open enclosure, where there were forty or fifty such pieces, and where labour was at its briskest when the hired labour of the day had ended. Digging began usually at six o'clock, and extended indefinitely into the dusk or moon-light.'

Where the allotments were supplied by the local squire or the rector there were often rules such as those printed for Upwey in 1837: '1: No work whatever to be done on the Sabbath, on pain of forfeiture of the crop, and immediate deprivation of the allotment.' The other four rules concern rent, and keeping the allotment and paths tidy, concluding 'No tenant will be removed, so long as he *maintains a character for honesty, sobriety, and general good conduct*' (and obeys all the rules!). In Puddletown no work at all, even in gardens, was allowed on Sundays. With labourers then working a full six-day week these rules must have made it difficult ever to get any land dug.

When Hardy was young, many people were still making their

own cider. He helped his father to make their family supply at Bockhampton for most years until 1873: 'a proceeding he had always enjoyed from childhood . . . a work whose sweet smells and oozings in the crisp autumn air can never be forgotten by those who have a hand in it.' Some people employed travelling cider-makers, like Giles Winterborne in *The Woodlanders*, who had 'a press and mill fixed to wheels instead of being set up in a cider-house' and who wandered from place to place pressing the countless especially-grown varieties of sour cider-apple. 'He looked and smelt like Autumn's very brother . . . His sleeves and leggings dyed with fruit-stains . . . his hat sprinkled with pips.' In *Under the Greenwood Tree* cider made at Mellstock (Stinsford/Bockhampton) is described as 'a real drop o' cordial from the best picked apples – Sansons, Stubbards, Five-corners, and such-like . . . a sprinkling of they that grow down by the orchard rails'.

Until the later nineteenth century most occupations had distinctive clothing, so that it was possible to distinguish for example a mason from a shepherd – the former wearing a long linen apron, the latter wearing a smock and carrying a crook. In Hardy's youth most workers on the land wore smocks, elaborate over-shirts with much embroidery, and kept a suit for Sundays and holidays. When Gabriel Oak visits Bathsheba at the start of *Far from the Madding Crowd* he 'took a new handkerchief from the bottom of his clothes-box, and put on the light waistcoat patterned all over with sprigs of an elegant flower uniting the beauties of both rose and lily without the defects of either, and used all the hair-oil he possessed'. On weekdays, when a farmer, he 'wore a low-crowned felt hat . . . and a coat like Dr. Johnson's; his lower extremities being encased in ordinary leather leggings and boots emphatically large'. His watch was in a fob 'difficult of access, by reason of its somewhat high situation in the waistband of his trousers (which also lay at a remote height under his waistcoat)'. When he has to become a shepherd again, he exchanges his overcoat for a smock.

In *Under the Greenwood Tree* Reuben Dewy's good trousers are admired by his wife as 'lined inside, and double-lined in the lower parts, and an extra piece of stiffening at the bottom. And 'tis a nice high cut that comes right up under your armpits, and there's enough turned down inside the seams to make half a pair more.' Clothes for both men and women were made to last, and were

*A Dorset farm labourer, probably William Churchill, about 1897. His very worn smock is of blue linen which looks very much like denim.*

*Job Green, who worked as a shepherd in West Dorset, in an unusual short smock embroidered with the Prince of Wales Feathers on the front, probably in the 1880s. This smock, and another simpler one which also belonged to him, survive and are in the Dorset County Museum.*

formally graded by their wearers from best, second best, etc., down to work-clothes, with the correct grade brought out for every occasion. Gabriel Oak's visiting clothes were 'a degree between fine-market-day and wet-Sunday selection'. A man's wedding-coat would be carefully stored all his life, and brought out only for very special occasions. In *The Trumpet Major* Miller Loveday's best coat 'had seen five and twenty summers, chiefly through the chinks of a clothes-box, and was not at all shabby as yet, though getting singular. But that could not be helped; common coats and best coats were distinct species, and never interchangeable.'

In 1883, in *The Dorsetshire Labourer*, Hardy regrets the passing of 'the genuine white smock-frock of Russia duck and the

*Even when sent out to play, children wore their pinafores and hats.*

whity-brown one of drabbett' (duck and drabbet were respectively untwilled and twilled linen) and says that they are only seen 'on the shoulders of old men. Where smocks are worn by the young and middle-aged, they are of blue material . . . a mangy old coat is often preferred; so that often a group of these honest fellows on the

*This young mother wears the 'bright-hued neckerchief' and bonnet which Hardy says was disappearing in 1883. There is a strange contrast between the beautiful, still girl and the children, distorted because they have moved.*

arable has the aspect of a body of tramps.' Women's clothing was also changing: 'Instead of the wing bonnet like the tilt of a wagon, cotton gown, bright-hued neckerchief, and strong flat boots and shoes, they (the younger ones at least) wear shabby millinery bonnets and hats with beads and feathers, "material" dresses, and boot-heels almost as foolishly shaped as those of ladies of highest education.'

The field girls binding the corn in *Tess* 'wore drawn cotton bonnets with great flapping curtains to keep off the sun . . . There was one wearing a pale pink jacket, another in cream-coloured tight-sleeved gown, another in a petticoat as red as the arms of the reaping-machine; and others, older, in the brown-rough 'wropper' [wrapper] or overall – the old-established and most appropriate dress of the field-woman, which the younger ones were abandoning.'

All children except gypsies wore white aprons or pinafores that must have been horribly difficult to keep clean. Perhaps the greatest difference in clothes from today was the universal wearing of hats out of doors. Even children wore them: gypsy girls and women seem to be the only exceptions, judging from the photographs.

Clothing and coal clubs were sometimes set up to help the labourers and their families. The Commission on the Employment of Women and Children in Agriculture recorded a club in Blandford Forum in 1843. 'Any labouring family of good conduct' could belong, and subscribed between 1d to 3d (½p-1½p) a week. At Christmas 'these subscriptions are doubled by the donations of persons in a better position of life living in the neighbourhood'. Subscribers then spent the money at the shop of 'the tradesman appointed to supply the club'. The purchases had to be 'plain articles of dress or household linen'; it was 'an imperative rule of the club that if any subscriber purchases with club-money any articles of dress or linen not of a plain and useful description, he ceases to be a member.' Ill-conduct also prevented a person from remaining a member.

This Blandford club spent two thousand pounds during Christmas 1843, and like many Victorian charities must have been very beneficial. However, the restrictive clauses irritate, and are clearly there to satisfy both Church and middle-class donors. The Victorians liked to retain charity in private hands, so that they could distinguish between the people they regarded as the deserving poor, whom they helped, and the undeserving poor, whom they did not. Lack of respect for one's betters, drinking or other 'ill conduct' meant not only going without the plain and serviceable new clothes from the club, but also not benefiting from the many other private charities. In the mid-nineteenth century John Bright, the reformer, wrote that Dorset 'clothing and coal clubs are under the control of the Clergy, and are used for religious or political patronage'.

*John Dunford, thatcher and parish clerk, leader of the village band at Winterbourne Abbas, near Dorchester. He played the clarinet, his son the bass viol, and Richard Tompkins the flute. When the photograph was taken, in 1897, John Dunford was seventy-two and had played in the church band for forty-two years. He died that year, but his son continued playing in the church until 1940.*

*Under the Greenwood Tree* affectionately recorded the instrumental choir or band at Stinsford, which Hardy's father and grandfather had organised for forty years up to 1843. His grandfather played the bass viol, an early type of 'cello, and the band was completed by three violins, one played by Hardy's father. The band organised the singers, and really controlled all the music in the parish, religious and secular, as they also played at dances, weddings and other celebrations. As in the novel, the Stinsford choir was replaced by an organ when Hardy was only a small child, but they still kept up the Christmas carolling around the village and playing for dances while Hardy was a young man.

Puddletown had a larger band, including clarionets and serpents as well as string instruments. The Mellstock choir is scathing about others who include instruments other than string: ' "Clar-'nets were not made for the service of the Lard; you can see it by looking at 'em".' Their real opposition, however, is to the harmoniums and barrel organs which are threatening to replace them: 'Miserable dumbledores [bumble-bees]'.

According to *A Few Crusted Characters* the choirs could 'turn a jig or a hornpipe out of hand as well as ever they could turn out a psalm, and perhaps better . . . one half-hour they could be playing a Christmas carol in the squire's hall to the ladies and gentlemen, and drinking tay and coffee with 'em as modest as saints; and the next, at the Tinker's Arms, blazing away like wild horses with the "Dashing White Sergeant" to nine couple of dancers and more, and swallowing rum-and-cider hot as flame.' One Sunday this choir was tired after playing for 'one rattling randy [merry-making] after another'. They drank hot brandy and beer during the service, slept during the sermon, and when they awoke thought they were still at a randy and dashed into a dance tune. When there was little reaction from the congregation (it was a dark afternoon) the leader cried out 'Top couples cross hands and when I make the fiddle squeak at the end, every man kiss his pardner under the mistletoe.' They were immediately replaced by a barrel organ 'that would play two and twenty new psalm tunes . . . [with] a really respectable man to turn the winch.'

The Christmas carolling involved singing to every inhabitant of the village on Christmas Day itself, which in scattered hamlets meant a long walk. In the short story *The Grave by the Handpost* the choir realise that they have assembled before midnight on Christmas Eve, but then decided to start with some outlying cottages 'where people had no clocks' and so wouldn't know that they were being serenaded on Christmas Eve rather than Christmas morning. The Mellstock Choir have the horrible experience of being told to shut up by one of the farmers they carol, but by playing 'Fortissimy' they drown 'enough invectives to consign the whole parish to perdition'. They forgive his 'onseemly' behaviour because he's been drinking and is 'well enough when he's in his religious frame'.

Hardy himself played at village weddings, 'at one of which the bride, all in white, kissed him in her intense pleasure at the dance'.

58

*Robert Larcombe, parish clerk of
Blackdown.*

A jovial rural party is described in *Under the Greenwood Tree*, with the long country dances that Hardy and his father played. 'The party reached the period when ladies' back-hair begins to look forgotten and dissipated; when a perceptible dampness makes itself apparent upon the faces even of delicate girls – a ghastly dew having for some time rained from the faces of their masculine partners; when skirts begin to be torn out of their gathers; when elderly people, who have stood up to please their juniors, begin to feel sundry small tremblings in the region of the knees . . . when waistcoats begin to be unbuttoned, and when the fiddlers' chairs have been wriggled, by the frantic bowing of their occupiers, to a distance of about two feet from where they originally stood.'

In *The Return of the Native*, Timothy Fairway complains that 'a wedding at home means five- and six-handed reels by the hour; and they do a man's legs no good when he's over forty'. His companion replies, 'Once at the woman's house you can hardly say nay to being one in a jig, knowing all the time that you can be expected to make yourself worth your victuals.' Fairway replies that you have to dance 'at Christmas because 'tis the time o' year; you must dance at weddings because 'tis the time o' life. At christenings folk will even smuggle in a reel or two . . . For my part I like a good hearty funeral as well as anything. You've splendid victuals and drink as at other parties, and even better. And it don't wear your legs to stump in talking over a poor fellow's ways as it do to stand up in hornpipes.'

Many of Hardy's novels include descriptions of happy rural parties, which must reflect those he knew as a boy and young man. All his life he preserved in his study his father's violin and the old hand-written music books of the Stinsford choir.

The traditional drama was mumming, although the long ballads sung at all gatherings (like those at the sheep-shearing supper in *Far from the Madding Crowd*) were really dramatic narratives, as were many of the long stories from the past told round the fireside. The commonest spectator sport was close observation of neighbours' activities, combined with communal comment thereon.

Hardy describes mummers in a famous passage from *The Return of the Native*: 'The mummers themselves were not afflicted with any such feeling [contempt] for their art, though at the same time they were not enthusiastic. A traditional pastime is to be distinguished from a mere revival in no more striking feature than this, that while in the revival all is excitement and fervour, the survival is carried on with a stolidity and absence of stir.' Their audience at Mrs Yeobright's Christmas party accept the mummers' play just as casually. 'Nobody commented, any more than they would have commented on the fact of mushrooms coming in autumn or snowdrops in spring . . . It was a phase of cheerfulness which was, as a matter of course, to be passed through every Christmas.'

Hardy insisted that the Dorset dialect was not spoken in his parents' house, but his younger brother Henry is reported to have had a very broad accent, and Hardy himself talked to country people in an approximation of dialect, though normally speaking Standard English. His rustic characters use dialect, but he disagreed with the Dorset poet and philologist, William Barnes, about the best ways of reproducing it.  Many of Barnes' finest poems are in phonetically-spelt dialect, for example in 'The Geäte a-Vallen to' (the gate a-falling to). Initial *s* was pronounced as *z*, *f* as *v*; *hwome* represents the old long Anglo-Saxon vowel, still sometimes to be heard even today in remoter parts of the county.

> In the zunsheen ov our zummers
> > Wi' the hay time now a-come
> How busy wer we out a-vield
> > Wi' vew a-left at hwome
> When wagons rumbled out ov yard
> > Red wheeled wi' body blue
> As back behind 'em loudly slamm'd
> > The geäte a-vallen to.

In the introduction to his selection of Barnes's poetry Hardy wrote 'many persons suppose that when anything is penned in the tongue of the country-side, the primary intent is burlesque or ridicule, and this especially if the speech be one in which the sibilant has the rough sound, and is expressed by Z.' Hardy preferred a more subtle and more easily comprehended rendering of rustic speech, although like Barnes he regarded the Dorset dialect as 'being – or having been – a tongue, and not a corruption'. He wrote that 'if a writer attempts to exhibit on paper the precise accents of a rustic speaker he disturbs the proper balance of a true representation by unduly insisting upon the grotesque element: thus directing attention to a point of inferior interest, and

*An old couple outside their cottage near Beaminster in the late nineteenth century.*

diverting it from the speaker's meaning.'

Hardy's rustic dialogue is realistically and sympathetically presented, and although most of the spelling is made regular, he succeeds in reproducing the style of the dialect, as in *Far from the Madding Crowd*: ' "... for a wet of the better class, that brought you no nearer to the horned man than you were afore you begun, there was none like those in Farmer Everdene's kitchen. Not a single damn allowed; no, not a bare poor one, even at the most cheerful moment when all were blindest, though the good old word of sin thrown in here and there at such times is a great relief to a merry soul." "True", said the maltster. "Nater [Nature] requires her swearing at the regular times, or she's not herself; and unholy exclamations is a necessity of life." '

Hardy describes Elizabeth-Jane in *The Mayor of Casterbridge* ridding herself of the 'vulgar' dialect. 'It came to pass that for "fay" she said "succeed"; that she no longer spoke of "dumbledores" but of "humble-bees"; no longer said of young men and women that they "walked together", but that they were "engaged"; that she grew to talk of "graggles" [bluebells] as "wild hyacinths"; that when she had not slept she did not quaintly tell the servants next morning that she had been "hag-rid", but that she had "suffered from indigestion".'

Hardy was always interested in local words, and occasionally used them in his poetry, for example 'The Bride-night Fire'. ('Totties' are feet, 'gallied' means frightened, and 'tardle', entanglement. 'Fall' remained in the Dorset dialect long after 'autumn' had taken its place in normal British English.)

> Her light-tripping totties, her ten little toes,
> All bare and besprinkled wi' Fall's chilly dews,
> While her great gallied eyes through her hair hanging loose
> Shone as stars through a tardle of trees.

The great treasure trove of Dorset words is Barnes's *Glossary* (1863), which contains very useful words such as 'magoty' for being fanciful, fond of experiments and crotchety, and 'leaze' for a field not mown for hay and 'mead' for one that is.

A charming characteristic of the Dorset dialect is its lack of respect for gender, shown at its best in a conversation recorded late in the nineteenth century, when the reply to an enquiry about the new baby's health was, 'She be nicely, zur, if he weren't asleep I'd show 'ee it.' Tess 'spoke two languages; the dialect at home, more or less; ordinary English abroad and to persons of quality' and she reproduces this gender muddle perfectly: ' "Had it anything to do with father's making such a mommet of himself in thik carriage this afternoon? Why did 'er?" ' Lyme Regis had a famous phrase for those who had lost the old 'Darzet' voice. 'Yere, 'ee cas'n spake zo well as cou'st, ca'st?' (Here, you can't speak as well as you could, can you?)

Mobility, and the assumption that only one version of English was genteel or respectable, helped to reduce the proportion of people speaking the Dorset dialect, and universal education sped the process. In the twentieth century the wireless virtually completed the dialect's eradication, although some of its old richness can still occasionally be heard in deeply rural parts.

In the second half of the nineteenth century half the labour of Puddletown was employed in agriculture, whereas in England as a whole the average was less than twenty per cent. This high level of employment in agriculture was broadly true of the whole of Dorset, so that trades either served agriculture directly, like the millers or seed merchants; or made and sold goods to those working in agriculture, like the boot and shoe makers. By about 1860 Dorset's small cottage industries, like button making or lace-making, had been completely taken over by the northern factories, and only a few specialised crafts, such as rope-making at Bridport and flax-spinning at Burton Bradstock, remained.

In *The Dorsetshire Labourer* Hardy wrote that 'Villages used to contain, in addition to the agricultural inhabitants, an interesting and better-informed class, ranking distinctly above those – the blacksmith, the carpenter, the shoe-maker, the small higgler [dealer and carrier], the shopkeeper, . . . together with nondescript-workers other than farm-labourers . . . Many of these families had been lifeholders, who built at their expense the cottages they occupied.' Many landlords now 'pull down each cottage as it falls in' because they 'disapprove of those petty tenants who are not in the estate's employ . . . the occupants who formed the backbone of village life have to seek refuge in the boroughs.'

*This splendidly posed photograph looks like a Dutch painting – the mother is sewing, while one daughter holds a frail and the other a bundle of firewood. The small cage hung by the door is for a bird. A frail is made from plated rushes and was the type of basket taken to the fields for 'nammet', which means lunch. Barnes thought the word derived from noon-meat.*

63

Lifehold was the survival of a medieval form of land-holding, whereby the land is held by a lease agreed with the landowner for a period of usually three lives. These three people are named in the lease, and as they die further names have to be added, or else the

*Winterbourne Steepleton, about 1890, taken by Miles Barnes, the son of William Barnes, the Dorset poet.*

*Looking through the outskirts of Corfe towards the Castle in the 1880s.*

land and buildings revert to the landowner, as happened to Giles Winterborne in *The Woodlanders*.

Hardy's parents and grandparents held the cottage in which he was born at Bockhampton lifehold, but they were never refused renewal of their lease. *Under the Greenwood Tree* is set at 'Mellstock'/Bockhampton, and includes many small tradesmen like Hardy's parents. Reuben Dewy is a tranter or carrier, Robert Penny a boot and shoe maker, grandfather James a mason, and Mr Spinks an ex-teacher at night school (night schools appeared commonly before education became fully compulsory in 1880, to instruct children obliged to work for their families all day). The

*Building Bardolf Manor near Puddletown in 1895. The man with the jacket could be the architect and the other is a stone-mason. The scaffolding is of great timber poles lashed together.*

heroine Fancy Day is also a schoolteacher, like Hardy's two sisters. Hardy's grandfather, father, and brother Henry were all small builders. His father was always self-employed, and steadily employed more labourers and craftsmen during the nineteenth century. There were only two at the 1851 Census, but by 1871, eight men and a boy. The Hardys were therefore part of the more independent upper part of the villagers, although not so elevated as Hardy later made them out to be.

In mid-century many of the larger villages still contained enough craftsmen to be virtually self-sufficient. Houses were built from local stone, or of cob – which Hardy described as 'mudwall: really a composition of chalk, clay, and straw – essentially, unbaked brick. This was mixed up into a sort of dough-pudding, close to where the cottage was to be built, then thrown up by pitch-forks on to the wall, where it was trodden down, till a "rise" of about three feet had been reached all round the building. This was left to settle for a day or two, then another rise was effected.' When the full height was reached and 'the wall had dried out a

*The thatcher at work on Hangman's Cottage, Dorchester in 1912. Gertrude Lodge in* The Withered Arm *visits the hangman here 'in a lonely cottage by a deep slow river'.*

little the outer face was cut down to a fairly flat surface with a spade, and the wall then plastered outside and in'. The thatch projected sufficiently to prevent much rain running down the outer plaster. (*The Ancient Cottages of England*, 1927.)

The roofs were also of local material – straw or reed. The thatch was held in place with twisted spars of local hazel, and in many cases the timbers in the roof, the doors, the windows and their frames were made from local timber. Hardy said that these indigenous buildings were 'ousted by the now ubiquitous brick-and-slate' about the middle of the nineteenth century. The villages then depended on Welsh slate and bricks from southern Dorset or even further afield, and probably used imported timber as well.

67

There was a considerable trade to the Dorset ports in Baltic timber all through the century, and Russian and Scandinavian ships were a familiar sight. At Lyme Regis the Russian sailors favoured one backstreet beerhouse, apparently because of its skittle alley.

Carts and wagons were also made in the villages, even down to the complex iron-shod wheels, which were made by the wheelwrights along with the rest of the vehicle. This led to great variation in style, shape, and even size, as each area made the variety best suited to its topography – where it was very hilly, lighter two-wheeled carts were preferred to the heavier wagons with four wheels. In Dorset wagons were generally small and heavily built compared to other counties.

*This smithy at Evershot in central Dorset belonged to Miss Jane B. Pullman from the 1870s to about 1910. The 1859 directory gives Mrs Ann Pullman as the blacksmith, so Jane was probably her daughter. These are doubtless her employees, apart from the man standing on the right who must have led the horse to the smithy. The man on the left appears to be dismantling a farm roller.*

68

A well-equipped smithy, probably in one
of the Dorset towns, in the 1880s. It was
probably described as an ironworks,
since it has not only a sophisticated forge,
but also a lathe, driven by an overhead
shaft. The iron fittings for carts and
wagons would have been made and
repaired here.

They were cheerfully painted, often in crimson and yellow or
blue, with their owner's name prominently on the tail-board. In
*Far from the Madding Crowd* one of the reasons Gabriel is
welcomed is because he can 'prent folks' names upon their wagons
almost like copper-plate, with beautiful flourishes, and great long
tails'. Again, from mid-century the local wheelwrights were being
challenged by the mass-produced carts and wagons, which by the
end of the century were becoming quite common.

The iron fittings for the earlier carts and wagons, and for the
cottages, were made by the local blacksmiths, who not only shod
horses but also made and repaired agricultural implements.
Despite the growth of specialist implement manufacturers and

cart-makers, blacksmiths still had plenty of work on the repairing side. In 1910-11 there were almost a million agricultural horses in England. This was the peak, but to this must be added all the carriage and riding horses. Working horses needed shoeing every two to four weeks, producing a lot of work.

The workshops of wheelwrights, blacksmiths, shoe makers and other craftsmen were the village meeting places for the men. The choir in *Under the Greenwood Tree* meet outside Mr Penny the shoe maker's workshop. Through the window Mr Penny can be seen at work 'facing the road with a boot on his knees and the awl in his hand'; in the background is 'an apprentice with a string tied round his hair . . . He smiled at remarks that floated in from without, but was never known to answer them in Mr Penny's presence.'

In *The Hand of Ethelberta* two of Beta's brothers decide to move from Dorset to London. Sol, a carpenter and joiner, is 'a very good staircase hand . . . neat at sash-frames . . . can knock together doors and shutters very well . . . and can do a little at the cabinet-making'; he does not mind framing a roof and is always ready to fill up his time 'at planing floor-boards by the foot'. His brother is equally adaptable and proficient, but they are advised that they both do too much to succeed in the city, 'where limitation is all the rule in labour'. To gain employment Sol 'must be a man who can thoroughly look at a door to see what ought to be done to it, but as to looking at a window, that's not your line'. Hardy obviously enjoyed parodying the differences he had found between town and country craftsmen when he moved to London.

Many villages had at least one mill for grinding the corn. Water-driven mills were also used for cloth production and to drive all sorts of machinery, though these were less common in the south outside towns. Most of Dorset's cloth mills, including two at Lyme and one in Dorchester, had closed during the 1840s in the face of northern competition. The corn mill in *The Trumpet-Major* is typical of many. It 'presented at one end the appearance of a hard-worked house slipping into the river, and at the other of an idle, genteel place, half-cloaked with creepers . . . two mill doors, one above the other, the upper enabling a person to step out upon nothing at a height of ten feet from the ground; a gaping arch vomiting the river . . . In the court at the front were two worn-out millstones, made useful again by being let in level with the

*This philosophical-looking shoemaker at Puddletown in 1899 was employed by Hardy's cousin, John Antell. Lea took a series of photographs of the cobbler in various poses: scratching his head over an impossibly worn-out boot, holding his work in a wooden vice between his knees, and – as shown here – finishing off a boot. The clutter about the workshop is amazing, and typical.*

The water mill at Lower Burton, near Dorchester, probably about 1880 when Edward Nutting was the miller. Everyone seems to have come out to be photographed: there is a light wagon and a single horse on the left with one of the millers; two women with babies and children; and another miller or more likely a carter with a heavier wagon drawn by two horses into which sacks, probably of flour, are being loaded. Yet another white-aproned man is seen to the right. The mill stream runs in the foreground, with chicken coops beyond.

ground. Here people stood to smoke and consider things in muddy weather; and cats slept on the clean surfaces when it was hot.' Inside the mills and mill-houses 'a subtle mist of superfine flour [gave] a pallid and ghostly look' to furniture, and the buildings were filled 'morning, noon, and night by the music of the mill, the wheels and cogs of which, being of wood, produced notes [which bore] a remote resemblance to the wooden tones of the stopped diapason in an organ. Occasionally ... there was added the cheerful clicking of the hopper', that was used to sieve the flour.

*In 1897 the owners of this superb
seventeenth century coaching inn at
Maiden Newton wanted to demolish it.
Hardy examined the building, and
suggested that it would be possible to
alter the rooms to suit modern
requirements. Sadly it was demolished
and replaced by a horrible half-timbered
building. In 1895 the White Horse was
advertising as a 'Commercial inn and
railway refreshment rooms'.*

Hardy loved the old coaching inns, and often visited them when out cycling or driving, much preferring them to the cafés and tearooms that began to spread after 1900. Many of his novels include an inn or pub of some sort. They were also important village and town meeting places. The malthouse in *Far from the Madding Crowd* is one of the humblest, not an inn but a place where barley was turned into malt for brewing. The barley was soaked in water, heated to make it germinate and then dried to stop the germination. The kiln used for the malting made Warren's malthouse a warm meeting place, where quantities of hot cider were drunk from the 'God-forgive-me', which was 'a two-handled tall mug . . . cracked and charred with heat . . . rather furred with extraneous matter about the outside . . . formed of ashes accidentally wetted with cider and baked hard'. It was called a God-forgive-me 'because its size makes any given toper feel ashamed of himself when he sees its bottom in drinking it empty'.

73

The huge mug was communal, passed from hand to hand. The old maltster had spent his life turnip-hoeing and harvesting in the summer, and malting in the winter. His malt would have been passed on to be ground, mixed with hot water and boiled with hops to make beer; or to farmers who would have brewed their own ale. The maltster's home in the novel was his workshop, and always had a sweet heavy smell of malt.

*All the customers outside the Sun Inn, East Street, Beaminster, about 1900. Mr S. Russell the landlord, is seen on the left with his wife and daughter. Only two of the drinkers have glasses – the others have pottery mugs.*

74

*The Ship Inn at Upwey in the 1890s, with a shepherd and his dog driving a small flock of sheep. This is the inn where Dick and Fancy in* Under the Greenwood Tree *stop to have tea on their way back from Weymouth, and become engaged.*

Rolliver's Inn, which Tess's parents frequented, was a little higher up the scale, although it had only an off-licence (allowing it to sell only for consumption elsewhere) and customers were served illegally in a bedroom. The landlady greeted every arrival with ' "Being a few private friends I've asked in to keep up club-walking at my own expense".' She was afraid 'it might be some gaffer [official person] sent by Gover'ment'.

Many of the larger inns were in the towns, and needed by country people when they went to market. Giles Winterborne in *The Woodlanders* realises too late that he should not have ordered lunch for Grace at the 'little tavern in a side street' that he generally uses when he goes to market. It was 'a long low apartment, with a sanded floor, herringboned with a broom, a wide, red-curtained window to the street, and another to the garden'. Grace has been accustomed to the best hotel in the town, and is not happy to sit 'on the well-scrubbed settle, opposite the narrow table, with its knives and steel forks, tin pepper-boxes, blue salt-cellars, and posters advertising the sale of bullocks against the wall'.

Dorchester was an important brewing town. Casterbridge strong beer 'was of the most beautiful colour . . . full in body, yet brisk as a volcano; piquant, yet without a twang; luminous as an autumn sunset; free from streakiness of taste; but, finally, rather heady . . . Anybody brought up for being drunk and disorderly in the streets of its natal borough, had only to prove that he was a stranger to the place and its liquor to be honourably dismissed by the magistrates, as one overtaken in a fault that no man could guard against who entered the town unawares.' It is to be hoped that Hardy remembered this when, four years after it was published in 1880, he became a Justice of the Peace in Dorchester.

In the nineteenth century most trades and crafts were in the hands of men, and only in shopkeeping and dressmaking are women found in charge. Often the shopkeeping was on a small scale. At Puddletown in 1859 the *Directory* lists 11 women in the 'commercial' section – 4 dressmakers, a milliner, 2 shopkeepers, a baker, 2 schoolmistresses and a postmistress. When women owned other businesses this was usually because they had taken over from their father, husband, or other male relative, like Bathsheba Everdene in *Far from the Madding Crowd*, who took over her uncle's farm when he died. Lower down the social scale, Marty South in *The Woodlanders* made spars when her father was ill, and took over Giles Winterborne's travelling cider press after he died.

Many women worked in agriculture, but usually in humble jobs. In the eighteenth and early nineteenth centuries a number had been occupied in rural industries such as spinning, lace-making and button-making, but most of these jobs had disappeared with the introduction of machinery, and the trades were transferred to the industrial north. Button-making machinery, for example, was introduced in 1851, and the button industry in Dorset was ruined. Between eight hundred and one thousand people had been employed by one firm alone, and many were forced to emigrate for lack of work. The majority of women did not work full-time, but with men's wages so pitifully low, part-time wages could make the difference between starvation and survival. A few cottage industries did survive through the nineteenth century, such as glove-making in north and east Dorset, but generally industrialisation meant that the area lost the industry altogether.

Many women, like Hardy's mother, went into service as maids, cooks or housekeepers, while those who had some education

*Great Fawley School, Berkshire, where Jude 'crazy for books' attended night school. He was employed during the day as a bird-scarer, being paid sixpence a day. One of Hardy's grandmothers came from Great Fawley.*

became governesses. The best opportunities for women in the nineteenth century lay in education, with the establishment of schools over the whole country. Most of the teachers were women.

From 1833 the government was making grants for new school buildings to two voluntary societies. The most widespread was the National Society for Promoting the Education of the Poor in the Principles of the Established Church in England and Wales, which, as its name implies, was aggressively Anglican. Indeed many National schools were founded more for evangelical and socio-political reasons that out of pure love of education. The Vicar of Lyme applied for a grant almost at once in 1833, but was refused; however, he immediately raised the money from 'parish charitables' and had a school building open – at a cost of £204 – by the autumn of 1834. But he insisted that the Church of England catechism be taught, which (as widely elsewhere) drove the outraged chapel meetings to build their own 'British school' only three years later.

Hardy began his own education at the Bockhampton National school. As at Lyme, its building had been partly financed by charity, in the form of Mrs Julia Martin, the wife of the owner of the Kingston Maurward estate on which the Hardys lived. Hardy recorded that 'she made it her hobby, till it was far superior to an ordinary village school'. It opened in 1848, and 'by a curious coincidence' Hardy was 'the first pupil to enter the new school-building, arriving on the day of opening, and awaiting tremulously and alone, in the empty room, the formal entry of the other scholars . . . from the temporary premises'.

In 1850 Hardy was transferred to the British school in Dorchester, run by the other society to receive government grants, the British and Foreign School Society. This was non-denominational, but received much support from non-conformists. The headmaster was 'an exceptionally able man' according to Hardy, who recalled that he 'did not know till he had been there several months that it was a non-conformist school . . . a large number, probably a majority, of the boys coming like himself from Church-of-England homes'.

Unfortunately Mrs Martin took a less enlightened view of Hardy's transfer to what she regarded to be (religiously) the wrong sort of school and employed another firm to do building and repairs about the estate – in place of Hardy's father, who had previously done the work. Another common type of village or small town school was the dame school for the very young, usually the children of parents who felt themselves a cut above the infants' class in the National or British schools. Dame schools continued in many places up to 1900 and even beyond. As the name suggests, the mistress was usually an old woman or a widow. Hardy's Puddletown aunt, Mary Antell, ran a dame school there.

The Education Act of 1870 established schools in the gaps left between the schools of the voluntary societies, ensuring that elementary education was available all over the country. These new schools were paid for by local government, and were called Board schools because they were run by locally elected School Boards. From 1870 local authorities could make education compulsory in their areas, but full national compulsion only came in 1880, when all children had to attend school up to the age of ten.

This was difficult to enforce as, together with many of the upper classes and farmers, some parents could not see that children who

*Children on their way to school with their slates, 1890s.*

*These two boys seem to be enjoying being photographed, whilst a third stays in the background.*

*The annual children's treat at Bardolf Manor in about 1896. These are the children of the estate workers, but school tea-parties looked very similar. All the girls have their best dresses and boaters on.*

were going to be labourers or servants needed education. At a meeting of the Blandford Board of Guardians in 1868 one of them roundly declared 'that the less education labourers have the better' and he was duly applauded. The wife of a shepherd from Blandford (who had twelve children 'that lived') supplied the reason why. During the same year, she said of her sons 'they like to be good scholars, because it helps them to go away.' The furze-cutters in *The Return of the Native* complain that 'there's too much of that sending to school in these days! It only does harm. Every gatepost and barn's door you come to is sure to have some bad word or other chalked up on it by the rascals . . . Their fathers couldn't do it, and the country was all the better for it.'

The majority of children did attend school, but among the poorest absenteeism was high. At Puddletown in the 1880s children were kept away to plant potatoes, help with the harvest, look after babies, and in one case because their shoes were at the cobbler's and they had no others to come in. Even as late as 1899 the master at Burton Bradstock in West Dorset would cane children who appeared shoeless: poverty was no excuse. Other children were sent home from school because they had ringworm

*Reading aloud in a cottage at Puddletown in the 1890s. Possibly the old man cannot read. As a young man Hardy wrote love letters for village girls who could not write, but who had sweethearts in India.*

or lice in their hair. The number of children at school over the whole country increased from one and a quarter million in 1870 to four and half million in 1890.

Until 1902 parents had to pay for their children to go to school. In Dorset the fees varied from one penny to fourpence a week, sometimes with reductions if more than one child from the same family was at school.

Both Hardy's sisters trained as teachers at Salisbury training college, and both disliked it, especially the younger sister, Kate. Hardy shows it rather unsympathetically in *Jude* as a 'species of nunnery'. It was 'a very mixed community, which included the daughters of mechanics, curates, surgeons, shopkeepers, farmers, dairymen, soldiers, sailors, and villagers.' With the need for so many teachers it was possible for a village girl, if clever, to train as

*A ford in Dorset, taken by Lea in the 1890s. Several minor roads in Dorset still cross shallow rivers in this way. Carts and wagons were driven into rivers in hot weather to swell the wooden spokes of their wheels.*

*Another photograph of the annual treat at Bardolf Manor.*

a teacher and earn four or five times as much as her labouring father as soon as she left college. Hardy's cousin, Tryphena Sparks, an important figure in both his emotional and imaginative life, became a headmistress directly from college, having been a pupil-teacher at Puddletown school.

Fancy Day in *Under the Greenwood Tree* did well enough at school to receive a grant to go to training college, and emerged from it with 'the highest of the first class' certificates for teaching. All would-be teachers had a five-year apprenticeship as pupil-teachers from the age of thirteen to eighteen. This could be followed either by a period at training college, or if the entrance examination for college was failed, by taking an examination for a teacher's certificate after teaching for some years. Hardy's second wife, Florence Dugdale, trained by this second method.

Most of the nineteenth-century legislation was for elementary education, secondary schooling being left to the private and the old grammar schools until the twentieth century. Hardy was lucky to transfer to the new British school set-up in Dorchester by its headmaster. He received a good education up to the age of sixteen, when he left to be apprenticed to a Dorchester architect.

Church and chapel remained an important part of village life all through the century, even though the 1851 Census showed that, on the Sunday before it was taken, less than half the adult population had been to either. The Church of England vicar or rector ranked socially only just below the local squire. There was an immense variety of local clergy, from the Tory die-hard to the earnest evangelical, from the considerable scholar-scientist such as William Barnes or Octavius Pickard-Cambridge, vicar of Bloxworth near Dorchester (a major authority on spiders), to the hellfire preachers of many a chapel. Some, such as the Reverend F. P. Hodges, vicar of Lyme from 1833 to 1870, almost defeat our understanding. Hodges was a fierce autocrat, and all through his life wore for formal occasions the jabot and silk stockings of his youth. He very soon killed off an old tradition of Lyme, caused by its steep streets, the walking funeral; letting his parishioners know that no carriages, no vicar. His nickname was 'The Bishop of

Lyme'. Yet he was an evangelist and the town owes him its first public education in the 1830's; he was the driving force behind the schools, both spiritually and financially . . . as long as his own church's catechism was taught. He would not give an inch to the dissenters.

Many villages were caught between these paradoxical strains in the Victorian clergy – the gentlemen descendants of the eighteenth-century church, and the eternal harrying by evangelical curates and ministers, with their temperance crusades and the rest. The church bazaar became a popular way of raising money for good causes, among the more educated. No doubt a great deal of genuine charity was performed, both personally and as church members; but there hangs over much of it, as Hardy suggests, an odour of good deeds done more for self-interested reasons – encouraging the working classes to put up with their lowly station – rather than for true Christian ones.

There were exceptions, however. The aristocratic Sidney Godolphin Osborne (1808-1889), rector of Durweston near Blandford from 1841 to 1875, and brother-in-law of the novelist Charles Kingsley, campaigned on behalf of the Dorset labourer all his life, publishing fierce letters regularly in *The Times*, giving evidence to the Royal Commissions on Agriculture, and even lecturing to Farmers' Clubs. He was very outspoken, and to begin with very unpopular. He said he was 'content to be condemned as an officious, dangerous meddler with the peace of this country . . . my conscience is at ease'. He helped many labourers to emigrate or to get better jobs.

In *Under the Greenwood Tree* the choir complain that their old vicar never came ' "mumbudgeting [silencing] you . . . just when you were in the middle of your work" '; but with their new enthusiastic vicar, ' "as to sifting your cinders, scrubbing your floors, or emptying your soap-suds, why, you can't do it . . . for as sure as the sun you meet him at the door, coming to ask how you be, and 'tis such a confusing thing to meet a gentleman at the door when ye are in the mess o' washing" '. They decide ' "'tis only for want of knowing better . . . your pa'son comes by fate: 'tis heads or tails, like pitch-halfpenny, and no choosing".'

Stinsford, the church closest to his birthplace, was the one most frequently visited by Hardy. His father and grandfather had played the violin and bass viol in the church choir until a year

'Bathsheba Everdene in church' is the original caption to this. It was set up by Hermann Lea in Puddletown church about 1901, with an artist's model dressed in mid-nineteenth century clothes – the period of the novel. This represents no particular scene in Far from the Madding Crowd, *but doubtless Lea wanted to show the splendid fittings of the church in the photograph.*

after he was born, and he recorded his mother's first seeing the choir there, about 1835, in the poem 'A Church Romance'.

> She turned in the high pew, until her sight
> Swept the west gallery, and caught its row
> Of music-men with viol, book and bow
> Against the sinking, sad tower-window light . . .

Sixty years later he remembered his own childhood at the church, in 'Afternoon Service at Mellstock, *c.* 1850'.

> We watched the elms, we watched the rooks
>       The cloud upon the breeze,
> Between whiles of glancing at our books,
>       And swaying like the trees
> So mindless were those outpourings: –
>       Though I am not aware
> That I have gained by subtle thoughts on things
>       Since we stood psalming there.

As a young child Hardy would dress up in a tablecloth and play

*Tess saw gates and stiles with painted texts from the scriptures, and asked Alec (in his brief evangelical phase) who had been 'at the pains to blazon these announcements. He told her that the man was employed . . . to paint these reminders that no means might be left untried which might move the hearts of a wicked generation.'*

at being a vicar conducting services. As a young man he was a regular, thoughtful church-goer, and in his twenties he apparently considered reading for a degree at Cambridge so that he could take orders. However he gradually became a famous agnostic, with a lack of faith except in a blind or a Darwinian fate (Hardy said he was 'among the earliest acclaimers of *The Origin of Species*', published in 1859). This was reflected in many of his novels – especially *Jude the Obscure* and *Tess of the D'Urbervilles*, and also in poems such as 'God's Funeral', or 'Nature's Questioning':

"Has some Vast Imbecility,
    Mighty to build and blend,
    But impotent to tend,
Framed us in jest, and left us now to hazardry?

Or come we of an Automaton
    Unconscious of our pains? . . .
    Or are we live remains
Of Godhead dying downwards, brain and eye now gone?"

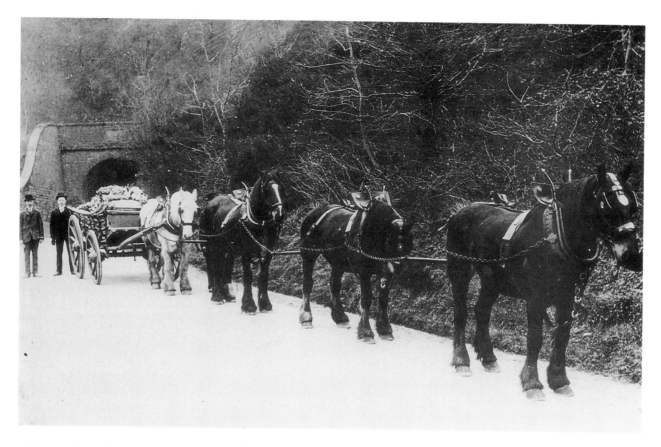

These fiercely doubting poems have to be balanced against
others, like 'The Oxen'.

>             . . . Yet, I feel,
>         If someone said on Christmas Eve,
>             'Come; see the oxen kneel
>
>         In the lonely barton by yonder coomb
>             Our childhood used to know,'
>         I should go with him in the gloom,
>             Hoping it might be so.

He regularly visited Stinsford in his old age, because his
parents, sister and first wife were buried there. He thought he
would be buried there too, but despite the specific instructions in

*The funeral of the Reverend Paulet
Mildmay Compton on March 2nd, 1906.
The Dorset County Chronicle reported
that it was the deceased's 'express wish
that he should be conveyed to his last
resting place' by horse and wagon. His
coffin was covered with bunches of
primroses, and 'placed in a farm wagon,
which was drawn by four cart horses,
three bays and a white. . . . At the heads
of the first and third horses a carter in
black clothes walked.' The wagons
carried him from Mapperton, where he
had been living since 1848, to Crewkerne,
nine miles away, where 'a special train
had been engaged to take the body, horses
and wagon, and mourners, to Romsey'.
After the sixty-five miles by rail the
'quaint procession' proceeded by road to
Minstead, where he was buried.
According to family tradition, Jo
Draper's great-great-grandfather,
George Godwin, was head gamekeeper at
Minstead at this period and must have
attended the funeral.*

*Funerals using carts rather than
hearses were strange by 1906, but in the
earlier nineteenth century they were
common. Fanny Robin in* Far from the
Madding Crowd *is carried from the
workhouse to her grave in one.*

his will only his heart was interred in Dorset. The ashes of the rest of his body are in Westminster Abbey. In 'A Refusal' Hardy made the 'grave dean' of Westminster Abbey, who had just refused to have Byron's ashes in his church, say:

> When bent on enshrining
> Rapscallions, and signing
> Their names on God's stonework
> As if like his own work
> Were their lucubrations:
> And passed is my patience
> That such a creed-scorner
> (Not mentioning horner)
> Should claim Poet's Corner!

Horner is an obsolete word for a Casanova.

When he attended the novelist Meredith's memorial service in Westminster Abbey in 1909 Hardy stated himself 'put into a saintly niche which I felt I desecrated'. He thought that there should be 'a heathen annexe to the Abbey, strictly accursed by the Dean and clergy on its opening day to hold people like Meredith, Swinburne, Spencer &c'. He also thought that if writers left specific instructions as to where they should be buried, the problem would not arise. It is therefore particularly ironic that his own specific instructions were ignored and that he should end at least in part in Westminster Abbey. T. E. Lawrence wrote that 'Hardy was too great to be suffered as an enemy of their faith: so he must be redeemed.' A fortnight before he died he asked his wife to read him the gospel accounts of the nativity, and commented afterwards that there was not a grain of evidence that the gospel story was true in any detail.

There are many clergymen in Hardy's fiction, but except in a couple of short stories they are not major characters. In two cases Hardy was criticised for cynically producing unsympathetic clergymen. The bishop in *Two on a Tower* is not only palmed off with someone else's son, but presented as a pompous fool. In *Tess of the D'Urbervilles* the vicar refused to bury Tess's baby, so that the infant was 'buried by candle-light . . . in that shabby corner of God's allotment where He lets the nettles grow; and where all unbaptised infants, notorious drunkards, suicides, and others of the conjecturally damned are laid'. Both these clergymen provoked a hostile reception, driving Hardy to defend himself as to the

*Ibberton Church about 1890, after the partial collapse of the building. It was restored in 1902.*

possibility of such things having happened, and claiming in a later introduction to *Two on a Tower* that 'the Bishop is every inch a gentleman'.

The novel that expressed the most anti-Christian views was *Jude the Obscure*: Sue, the heroine, characteristically declares ' "I'd rather sit in the railway station . . . That's the centre of the town life now. The Cathedral has had its day!" ' One newspaper suggested it was written by Hardy the Degenerate, while the Bishop of Wakefield claimed to have burnt *Jude* in disgust. Hardy pointed out that since it was a good thick book, and the middle of summer, this must have been quite difficult. He wrote to a friend 'theology and burning (spiritual and temporal) have been associated for so many centuries that I suppose they will continue allies to the end.'

*Inside Turnworth church about 1900, showing the rather strange low pillars. Hardy designed the elaborate carved decoration of the capitals.*

Hardy was not rabidly anti-clerical, and was friends with several clergy and religious people. The Reverend Thomas Perkins was a good friend of his, as was the religiously minded curator of the Dorset County Museum, Henry Moule. He did however make one of the clergymen in the short story *A Tragedy of Two Ambitions* say, 'To succeed in the Church, people must believe in you, first of all, as a gentleman, secondly as a man of means, thirdly as a scholar, fourthly as a preacher, fifthly, perhaps, as a Christian.'

*Stratton Church in 1894, with the restoration just beginning. Hardy fought against the restoration of this church, which involved demolishing most of the building, apart from the tower. He succeeded in having the original windows and doors re-set in the new building.*

Hardy had a remarkable familiarity with the Bible, and quotations from it are common in his prose and poetry. As a young man he had read much of the New Testament in Greek. He later described himself as 'churchy' and a 'harmless agnostic'.

Hardy trained as an architect at a period when church restoration was at its height. Between 1840 and 1876, 158 out of about 300 parish churches in Dorset were restored or rebuilt, costing from £500 up to many thousands. In 'Memories of Church Restoration', a lecture given to the Society for the Protection of Ancient Buildings in 1906, he stated sadly that 'if all the mediaeval buildings in England had been left as they stood [about 1825] . . . to incur whatever dilapidations might have befallen them at the hands of time, weather and general neglect, this country would have been richer in specimens today than it finds itself to be after the expenditure of millions in a nominal preservation during that period.' He recalled that really thorough restoration had involved completely pulling down churches, while others were made 'more uniform by removing the features of all but one style, and imitating that throughout in new work'. Although this no longer happened in 1906, church maintenance, never mind restoration, was still fraught with difficulties because 'the building is beheld in two contradictory lights, and required for two incompatible purposes. To the incumbent the church is a workshop or laboratory; to the antiquary it is a relic. To the parish it is a utility; to the outsider a luxury.'

There is no doubt that many churches were in need of maintenance. Ibberton, which must have been visited by Hardy when cycling with the Rev. Thomas Perkins, whose own church at Turnworth is only three miles away, had to be abandoned in the later nineteenth century because it was in such bad condition. A temporary church of corrugated iron was built. It was lucky for Ibberton that the restoration was not carried out until 1902, as by that time architects were much more sensitive and the church was restored properly rather than rebuilt.

Perkins' Turnworth suffered a much worse fate at the hands of the architect. As a memorial to the local squire the church was 'restored' in 1868 by having the whole church (except the tower) demolished and rebuilt in the then 'correct' fourteenth-century gothic style. It was designed by John Hicks of Dorchester and built by G. R. Crickmay. The rebuilding was supervised by Thomas Hardy.

Stratton Church met a rather similar fate, but by 1889, when it was threatened by the 'restorer', Hardy had been converted to a more sensitive approach, and alerted the Society for the Protection of Ancient Buildings to the threat. Between them they managed to save many of its original features.

Hardy wrote several reports on threatened buildings after he had stopped practising as an architect, giving good advice on maintenance. He was upset by proposals to demolish the chancel of Puddletown Church, because the local squire thought it 'quite out

*The church at Puddletown (Weatherbury of* Far from the Madding Crowd*), about 1900, before the cottages (such as that seen on the right) were demolished to provide stone for its extension.*

of proportion to the rest of the church'. Hardy again alerted the Society for the Protection of Ancient Buildings, who inspired articles in *The Times* and *Country Life*, and produced a 'loud and powerful chorus of disapproval'. Puddletown was the Weatherbury of *Far from the Madding Crowd* and Hardy suggested that this could be used to enlist public sympathy 'even though we suppose it bestowed for foolish reasons'. The campaign failed, and in 1911 the chancel was rebuilt on a much grander scale, with materials obtained by demolishing an old cottage in the village. The unspoiled small Norman church of Winterborne Tomson, between Puddletown and Wimborne, was carefully restored in 1931 in memory of Hardy; and financed by the sale of his correspondence with, and reports written for the Society for the Protection of Ancient Buildings, which raised over £1,000.

Hardy was brought up with all the local superstitions and customs, incorporating many in his writing. He told J. S. Udal, the author of *Dorsetshire Folklore* (1922), that in his fiction he was 'careful not to falsify local beliefs and customs'.

Many of the customs were seasonal celebrations, like the May-day revels. In *The Return of the Native* the maypole is set up on the green outside Thomasin's window. 'At the top of the pole were crossed hoops decked with small flowers; beneath these came a milk-white zone of Maybloom; then a zone of bluebells, then of lilacs, then of ragged-robins, daffodils and so on . . . the enthusiastic brass band arrived and struck up . . . with apparently wind enough among its members to blow down the house.' *Tess of the D'Urbervilles* opens with a May-day dance which combines dancing with club-walking. By the nineteenth-century most of these clubs were really friendly societies, whose main purpose was to help their members save money, but many of them had a long history. Club-walking day was their feast day, with a parade around the parish, dancing and often a dinner.

Midsummer Eve was dedicated to several charms for discovering a girl's future husband. In *The Woodlanders* the village girls go deep into the woods to sow hempseed, a rite which traditionally revealed the husband. In the novel the spell is made more effective by all the village knowing what was going on, so that their sweethearts lurk in the bushes to capture the girls. Digging a hole at noon on Midsummer Day, a girl would hear her husband's trade.

Bonfires on November 5th 'were rather the lineal descendants from jumbled Druidical rites and Saxon ceremonies than the invention of popular feeling about Gunpowder plots. Moreover to light a fire is the instinctive and resistant act of man when, at the winter ingress, the curfew is sounded throughout nature.' *The Return of the Native* shows villagers of all ages enjoying the fires, and many of these seasonal customs were happy, if rowdy, communal events.

The figure customarily burnt on Bonfire Night was not, in many places with a dissenting tradition, that of Guy Fawkes, the Gunpowder Plot conspirator, but of the 'Pwup' or Pope, his supposed master. Lyme Regis went in for tar-barrel rolling on this night – barrels of tar and oily rags were set alight and guided with poles helter-skelter down its steep streets to a final bonfire. In 1902 the barrels were deliberately guided into the new shopfront of a butcher suspected of being pro-Boer, and ruined it. But the next year he became mayor of Lyme, and banned the ancient ceremony for ever. It continues today in several Devon towns.

Witches and conjurers were less happy phenomena. *The Return*

*The Jubilee equivalent of club-walking: the 400 children of Corfe Castle parading through the streets with their banners, wearing sashes and medals, led by the Rector. The local paper reports 'At three the children sat on the grass [in the Castle] and were regaled with a bountiful tea . . . the caterers gave general satisfaction.' The houses are described as 'tastefully trimmed in various ways'.*

*of the Native* shows Eustacia Vye being taken for a witch by Susan Nonsuch, who thinks Eustacia has cast a spell over her young son. Susan stabs Eustacia with a long needle in church, a traditional way of combating witches' power; and finally she makes a wax image of Eustacia, thrusts pins all through it, and burns it on the fire while repeating the Lord's prayer backwards. This time-honoured method of disposing of an enemy was successful: although no witch, Eustacia drowned the same night.

*Under the Greenwood Tree* includes a pleasant almost-witch who 'had a repute among women which was something between distinction and notoriety . . . She was shrewd and penetrating; her house stood in a lonely place; she never went to church; she wore a red cloak; she always retained her bonnet indoors; and she had a pointed chin . . . those who looked no further called her a witch. But she was not gaunt, nor ugly, nor particularly strange in manner; so that the term was softened, and she became simply a Deep Body, who was as long-headed as she was high.' She gives the heroine good, simple and effective advice, not spells or magic potions.

Conjurers were male witches, usually 'white' or beneficial. In *The Mayor of Casterbridge* Michael Henchard visits one to try to discover what the weather will be like for the harvest. Not only does Mr Fall correctly prophesy a bad harvest, but despite Henchard's disguise he knows him, and was expecting him.

Conjurers and witches also cured some ailments by advising sufferers to perform certain rituals. Warts could be charmed away by rubbing a piece of beef on the wart and then burying it. As the beef rotted the wart would fade away. The cure performed in *The Withered Arm* is much nastier. The heroine, Gertrude Lodge, is involuntarily 'overlooked' or bewitched by her husband's former mistress, causing one of her arms to wither. The conjurer says that it is 'the work of an enemy,' and she must 'touch with the limb the neck of a man who's been hanged', which will 'turn the blood and change the constitution'. He has sent dozens with skin complaints to the prison to do this. The hangman obliges. The hanged boy is the son of her husband and his former mistress, and the discovery of this, combined with 'the turn o' the blood', kills Gertrude.

As a young man Hardy saw two people hanged: executions were still popular public occasions in the middle of the nineteenth century. He always remembered seeing Martha Brown hung when he was sixteen (and 'stood close to the gallows'), recalling years later 'what a fine figure she showed against the sky . . . and how the tight black silk gown set off her shape as she wheeled half-round and back'. Hardy was very morbid, but so were most of his fellow country people.

Belief in witches was still very much alive in the first half of the nineteenth century. There was a remarkable case at Lyme in 1840, well recorded by George Roberts, the historian of the town. An old woman, Betty Trayt, was accused by an epileptic boy (as had happened often in the past), and was finally so persecuted that the magistrates had to protect her. A majority of the town believed the boy had been 'overlooked'. Various chapel ministers tried to exorcise him; a penny was collected from each of thirty virgins, in order to buy a prophylactic silver ring; it was even demanded that the poor old woman's blood be drawn with a rusty nail, a well-tried local recipe. Another was to hang a piece of bacon stuck with pins in a chimney (so the witch could not come down). Toads found in

*Warmwell Cross, near Owermoigne. Lonely cross-roads were traditionally used as burying spots for suicides, like the sergeant in the short story* The Grave by the Handpost. *They have a long association with bad luck, perhaps because they were where suicides and witches were always buried, and certainly because they were where the gibbets stood.*

houses were always taken out with the greatest gentleness and courtesy: they were witches' familiars, and must on no account be offended.

Belief in conjurers and witches died out towards the end of the nineteenth century, although many restricting or forecasting superstitions remained. Breaking a mirror, thirteen sitting down to a meal and many other things brought bad luck. Potents of death were also common, as in Hardy's poem 'Standing by the Mantelpiece'.

> This candle-wax is shaping to a shroud
> Tonight. (They call it that, as you may know) –
> By touching it the claimant is avowed,
> And hence I press it with my finger – so.

Bees were regarded as wise creatures. 'It was the universal custom hereabout to wake the bees by tapping at their hives whenever a death occurred in the household, under the belief that if this were not done the bees themselves would pine away and perish.' (*Interlopers at the Knap*). If bees belonging to the bride or groom swarmed on the wedding day it was lucky.

When Hardy was staying in Bath in 1902 his friend Henry Moule wrote to him about the Dorchester hare incident: 'a hare could think of nothing better to do than to run all up South Street, across Bull Stake, and up Pease Lane. At the top of the lane, opposite Miss A——'s stables, someone killed it. People who saw it,

*This doubly exposed photograph of Lea's shows a rather less serious attitude to the supernatural. Trick photography was common in the late nineteenth century: part of the plot of* A Laodicean *depends upon one. This is the same room seen on page 48, although Lea has moved the furniture around.*

or heard of it, said this vagary was a sure sign that there would be a fire here within a week. So certain of this was a fireman that he said he was half inclined not to go to bed last night . . ..' There was indeed a fire 'and of all places, at Miss A——'s stable. Soon put out it was . . . but some of our friends in the bottom of their hearts have, very likely, a thought that the ghost of the hare had something to do with it.' Townsmen were not immune to traditional beliefs, although they were less susceptible.

It might be added that a hare running up the main street of a town or village was a very old omen of an imminent fire. In pre-Christian times the hare was a holy creature, sacred to the Spring Goddess, the Anglo-Saxon Eastre – in that mythology Easter eggs were really hare's eggs. The Christian church, as with so many things, changed the hare's symbolic nature. It was above all feared and vilified as the animal witches preferred to change into, and could reputedly be killed only with a silver bullet. Even as late as 1913 a correspondent in *Notes and Queries* claimed there was a widespread dislike among Dorset country-people of eating the flesh of the animal, because of this association with witches.

The Chesil Bank fishermen were also highly superstitious. They never shot a seine-net on a Sunday, or harmed a seagull (for they held drowned sailors' souls). Their distinctive double-ended fishing boats (lerrets) always carried a holed, or holy, stone at bow and stern for luck: if this failed and the boat was bewitched, a dead mackerel was stuck with pins and brought aboard.

The vicar of Fordington when Hardy was at Max Gate, the patrician Grosvenor Bartelot, carefully started the restoration of the parish church of St George on 'the 7th day of the 7th month in the 7th year of the reign of King Edward the 7th' (1907). He also thought it was the seventh restoration. He wrote that 'with such a combination of sevens, I was quite certain of God's blessing.' The new nave was seven times twelve feet long, seven times seven feet broad, with seven windows on each side, and even each pillar was made of seven stones, and so on. Superstitions were clearly not limited to the labouring classes.

The labourers who worked the land owned very little of it, and
by the nineteenth century had even lost many of the rights over
common land which their forefathers had enjoyed, such as grazing
for their animals, gathering wood for domestic fuel and so on.
Surprisingly, only a few of the farmers owned land: most of them
were tenants. The land was owned by the upper classes – the
aristocracy, the gentry and the newly rich, most of whom did not
farm themselves. As Hardy records in *The Dorsetshire Labourer*

*The thatched castle, a late medieval sham, at Woodsford, where the young Thomas Hardy was tested in a survey by John Hicks, the architect who then took him on as a pupil. Hardy's father was one of the builders employed by Hicks to repair the building.*

this meant that 'the landowner, if he were good for anything, stood as a court of final appeal in cases of harsh dismissal of a man by a farmer. "I'll go to my lord" was a threat which overbearing farmers respected.'

The landowning class was small – a survey of 1872-3 showed that four-fifths of the land in Great Britain belonged to less than 7,000 people. Dorset particularly was a county of great estates. The same survey showed that seventeen families, mostly nobility, each held estates of over 7,000 acres in Dorset, owning between them 218,000 acres, or more than one-third of the county.

The upper classes were unmistakably distinct, their clothes, manners, speech and demeanour completely different from the middle or lower classes. They were formidably powerful. Anyone in Puddletown who did not conform to what Mr Brymer, the squire, wanted them to do had to leave the village; he owned almost all the houses, and controlled most of the jobs. The close social network among the gentry meant that if a labourer got a reputation for being a radical or too independent, he would find it very difficult to get work anywhere in the area.

The great landowners and the aristocracy not only controlled the land and those who worked on it, but until the later nineteenth century, the government also by becoming members of parliament themselves or by controlling their selection. Local affairs – the Poor Law Unions, the courts, and so on, including the County Councils when they appeared in 1888, were also run by them. They were seen as natural leaders by right of their birth and their breeding.

All the upper classes, including the nobility, gentry and clergy, received (and expected) absolute respect from the lower orders. Women curtsied and men touched their hat or pulled their forelock when they met their betters, although as Hardy recorded in *The Hand of Ethelberta* (1876) a more independent spirit was growing towards the end of the nineteenth century. ' "You'd be surprised to see how vain the girls about here be getting. Little rascals, why they won't curtsey to the loftiest lady in the land; no, not if you were to pay 'em to do it. Now, the men be different. Any man will touch his hat for a pint of beer. But then . . . touching your hat is a good deal less to do than bending your knees." '

Hardy did not belong to the upper classes, and his early experience of them was limited to the inhabitants of Kingston

*Kingston Maurward House from the lake. Built in brick in the early eighteenth century, it was later encased in stone – traditionally after George III regretted that it was only built of brick. Hardy recorded this story in* The Hand of Ethelberta, *where the house is described as 'a stone mask worn by a brick face'!*

Maurward House, on whose estate he lived, or more generally to gossip, and to information from his relatives and friends who were servants. His first novel (unpublished and now lost) *The Poor Man and the Lady* (1868) showed the upper classes in such a black manner that Alexander Macmillan, the publisher to whom it was submitted, wrote: 'It is inconceivable that any considerable number of human beings – God's creatures – should be so bad without going to utter wreck within a week.'

The young Hardy's resentment of the upper classes was shown rather crudely – Macmillan wrote: 'The utter heartlessness of *all* the conversation you give in drawing rooms and ballrooms about the working-classes, has *some* ground of truth I fear . . . but your chastisement would fall harmless from its very excess.' The upper-class father, whose daughter dies after he has refused to allow the poor man to marry her, is seen celebrating the fact that he has saved money because the poor man, an architect, has

*The entrance hall and the salon at Kingston Maurward House – worlds away from the Dorset cottages like the one Hardy's parents lived in on the estate belonging to this house.*

designed her monument for nothing. Macmillan thought Hardy 'meant mischief', and the novelist Meredith, who read the novel for the publisher, said it was 'a sweeping satire of the squirearchy and nobility, London society, the vulgarity of the middle class, modern Christianity, church restoration, and political and domestic morals in general . . . the tendency of the writing being socialistic, not to say revolutionary'.

Sparks of anger against the upper classes remain in a few of the other early novels, such as *The Hand of the Ethelberta*, but Hardy did not again produce bitter satire on the aristocracy. Marriages across class barriers are found in several of the novels, and Hardy is always as aware of the stratification within the upper classes, as he is within the lower.

In 1884 he returned to Dorchester as a successful novelist with nine books published, and started to receive and accept invitations from the aristocracy. Lady Portsmouth assured him that 'Ethelberta in his novel, who had been pronounced an impossible person by the reviewers, and the social manners unreal, had attracted her immensely because of her reality and naturalness . . . and that the society scenes were just as society was.' Hardy recorded this many years later, and was obviously pleased to refute the reviewers, and to have his knowledge of society confirmed by such a well-qualified source.

*The courtyard at Athelhampton, about 1886. It is probably Mr Wood-Homer who is turning the camera on Hermann Lea taking this photograph. His wife Eliza, who is standing next to him, was very friendly with the first Mrs Hardy, and their house (they had moved to Bardolf by then) was the last she visited before her death. The children are George and Christine Wood-Homer. Christine was to know both Hardy's wives, and to write* Thomas Hardy and his Two Wives.

*The fifteenth century hall at
Athelhampton, half a mile east of
Puddletown, after the restoration by
Alfred de la Fontaine, who lived there
from 1891 until 1918. Hardy was
friendly with him, and visited
Athelhampton quite often while he was
there. Hermann Lea lived there for a
short time from 1888 as a farm pupil of
Mr Wood-Homer, who lived in the house
from 1848 until 1891. The fireplace was
built by de la Fontaine, and later
removed. The ME on its plasterwork
stands for Elizabeth Martyn, wife of the
owner of Athelhampton between 1525
and 1550.*

Hardy seems always to have enjoyed being acquainted with
titled or old families. His first wife, Emma, was from the lower
gentry, a higher social class than he came from. She was the niece
of an archdeacon, a respectable connection that both she and
Hardy flourished at every opportunity. Emma found Hardy's
family difficult to get on with. She has been blamed for much of
Hardy's snobbery. However, he did not become noticeably more
egalitarian after she died, and was still careful to entertain his
brother and sisters only when there were no 'important' guests
present.

The upper part of the gentry and the nobility of the county migrated to London for 'the season' from April until early July, and the Hardys joined this exodus from the country from the early 1880s, generally renting a flat or staying in a hotel. Emma may have been the instigator, but Hardy certainly enjoyed mixing with 'society' and when Emma was too unwell to go he went on his own. While in London the Hardys had regular 'at homes' on Thursday afternoons, dispensing tea from an urn brought especially from Max Gate. Friends would drop in, or be invited to come. Hardy went to many concerts, and to the theatre a good deal while in London, and he and Emma went to many formal dinner parties. Hardy wrote of 'the contrasting planes of existence he moved in – vibrating at a swing between the artificial gaieties of a London season and the quaintness of a primitive rustic life'. After Emma's death in 1912 Hardy stopped going to London for the season, no doubt because of mourning, then of his remarriage in 1914 and the First World War. After 1918 he was probably too old (he was seventy-eight in that year) to want to go.

If Hardy enjoyed mixing with the upper classes during the London season, he did not enjoy many of their country pursuits. He hated blood sports and wrote 'the prevalence of those sports that consist in the pleasure of watching a fellow-creature, weaker and less favoured than ourselves, in its struggles to escape the death-agony we mean to inflict by a treacherous contrivance, seems to me one of the many convincing proofs that we have not yet emerged from barbarism.'

Many of the nobility, gentry and even clergy would have found this heresy. *Runs and Sporting Notes from Dorsetshire* by Henry Symonds, published in 1899, rejoices that 'this county has been from earliest records possessed in its resident Noblemen and Gentry, good men with strong proclivities for hunting...All honour to them.' The bulk of this book consists of dozens of descriptions of chasing otters, hares, deer and most importantly the fox, but it ends: 'to close this work without chronicling a deplorable fatal accident in the hunting field would be an incomplete *résumé* of the vicissitudes of the chase'. The death of Lord Guildford in 1885, aged thirty-four, is then detailed. His horse rolled over him after failing to take a fence: 'although severely injured he was conscious and said: "I could not keep his head down", alluding of course to the horse.' He died the next day.

*Charles J. Radclyffe (1839-1913), Master of Fox Hounds, of Wareham, Dorset, about 1870. He described his chief interest as 'sporting and agricultural', and would not dig out foxes which the hounds ran to earth, but left them 'for another day'. In the 1873-4 season his hounds hunted for fifty-seven days and killed forty-six foxes.*

*Waterston House, Bathsheba's farmhouse in* Far from the Madding Crowd; *'a hoary building, of the early stage of Classic Renaissance . . . Fluted pilasters, worked from the solid stone, decorated its front, and above the roof the chimneys were panelled or columnar, some coped gables with finials and like features still retaining traces of their Gothic extraction.' The centre of the house was rebuilt in 1863 after a fire. The right-hand wing is seventeenth century. Its elaborate decoration is dated 1586, but must have been brought from another house.*

The famous Squire Farquharson hunted over most of Dorset for fifty years from 1806, and in the twenty seasons from 1837 his pack hunted for 2,787 days and killed 2,688 foxes.

Hardy knew the largest Dorset land-owner, Augustus Henry Lane Fox, who added Pitt-Rivers to his already crowded name when he inherited an estate on Cranborne Chase in 1880. It comprised nearly twenty-five thousand acres in Dorset and almost three thousand more in Wiltshire, producing a gross income of £27,500 a year. Descended from the Pitts who owned Kingston Maurward in the eighteenth century, he was the first scientific archaeologist (described by Hardy in 1899 as 'one who has devotedly crawled amongst the stones [of Stonehenge] on his hands and knees inspecting rabbit holes, etc'), and spent some of his great wealth setting up museums, besides opening the Larmer pleasure grounds on his estate. The Larmer Grounds and his museums were open to the public, as he hoped that by demonstrating in the latter that steady evolution was a law of nature, he could convert the working classes from any thoughts of revolution. Hardy met his lovely daughter, Mrs (later Lady) Agnes Grove in the Larmer Grounds in 1895, and formed a romantic friendship with her. He advised her on her books, helped her to get her articles accepted by magazines, and corresponded with her until her death in 1926, when he wrote 'Concerning Agnes'.

I could not, though I should wish, have over again
> That old romance,
And sit apart in the shade as we sat then
> After the dance
The while I held her hand, and, to the booms
Of contrabassos, feet still pulsed from the distant rooms.

Hardy had an even more intense romantic and literary friendship from 1893 with another beautiful and aristocratic woman, Mrs Henniker, with whom he collaborated on a short story. Both relationships must have irritated his first wife, Emma, considerably.

The country houses of the upper classes ranged from huge buildings with wings and features of every date from late medieval to nineteenth century, like the Earl of Ilchester's house at Melbury (with a huge staff of indoor servants), which Hardy visited; down to small stone manor houses with perhaps five to ten servants. Bathsheba's house in *Far from the Madding Crowd* 'had once been the manorial hall upon a small estate . . . now altogether effaced as a distinct property'. Many manor-houses had become farms, or had been sold as houses with no land attached. The luxury found in all of them forms a sad contrast with the starkness of the labourers' cottages.

The upper classes were not static: the newly rich were continually adding to their number, especially in the nineteenth century when so many industrial fortunes were being made. Hardy was more interested in the descent to the working-class of old families. Tess's father, a tranter (small carrier), is told by an antiquarian that he is a D'Urberville, by rights Sir John D'Urberville; and Jack Durbeyfield is amazed to discover that he has 'ancistors – hundreds of 'em – in coats of mail and jewels, in gr't lead coffins weighing tons and tons. There's not a man in the county o' South-Wessex that's got grander and nobler skillentons in his family than I.' The family name has been taken up by 'an honest merchant (some said money-lender)' from the north who built himself a new mansion in the south; 'and in doing this he felt the necessity of recommencing with a name that would not too readily identify him with the smart tradesman of the past'. Ignorant of this, Tess the true D'Urberville (although corrupted to Durbeyfield) is sent to claim kinship, and her troubles start.

# Travel through Hardy's England

Travelling became easier during Hardy's lifetime. The train completely replaced road and much sea transport for long-distance travel, while later horse-drawn transport was challenged by cycles and motor-cars. Improvements mostly affected richer people and the carrying of goods. Walking remained a common means of getting from place to place, especially for the poor. Local travel was not affected so much by the railways, as they did not penetrate everywhere, especially in Dorset. Horse-drawn carriers from the villages continued to visit local towns two or three times a week, forming a main means of contact between the countryside and the towns.

Railways were being built before Hardy was born. In 1840, the year of his birth, the line from Southampton to London was opened, and in 1847 extended to Dorchester. It caused, according to Hardy, the loss of the traditional local songs, which were 'slain at a stroke by the London comic songs'; a side-light on the enormous changes brought about by railways.

Hardy travelled by train a good deal, especially to London. In the 1890s his letters from London show him intending to return to Dorchester by the 'usual' 6.13 or the 8.30. Many of his characters travel by train, most uncomfortably in the short story *The Fiddler of the Reels*. Car'line, the heroine, travels by an early (1851) excursion train from Dorset to London. 'The seats for the humbler class of travellers in these early experiments were open trucks, without any protection whatever from the wind and rain . . . the unfortunate occupants were found to be in a pitiable condition from their long journey; blue-faced, stiff-necked, sneezing, rain-beaten, chilled to the marrow.'

Other characters travel more comfortably, for example the hero and heroine of *Two on a Tower*, who go to Bath to be secretly married. In *A Pair of Blue Eyes*, Elfride and Stephen travel from Cornwall to London and back in one night, and the novel also includes Elfride's lovers, Stephen and Henry, travelling from London to Cornwall by train, not knowing that Elfride's coffin is in a special carriage attached to the back of the train.

The railways put most of the long-distance stage coaches out of business. The copy of the local paper announcing the opening of the

*Evershot station about 1890. This station opened in 1857, and in 1887 there were twelve stopping passenger trains on weekdays. Hardy used this station occasionally when returning from cycle trips.*

line from Yeovil to Dorchester in 1857 also includes an advertisement for the auction of '22 well-seasoned, powerful, fast, and well-bred coach-horses' and '3 well-built coaches', which had formed the coach service between Yeovil and Weymouth. With possibly unconscious irony the advertiser states that the sale is easy to get to, because of 'the various lines of railway now open to the town'. Towns on the railway routes increased in size, while those such as Beaminster or Cerne Abbas that were left off them, declined. Beaminster's population fell from 2,832 in 1851 to 1,702 in 1901; while Dorchester's population increased by a third during the same period.

It seems strange to us that throughout the nineteenth century horse-drawn transport and trains co-existed: because railways still survive they seem to belong to a later period. But horse-drawn carriages and carriers' wagons ran between places not on railway lines, while omnibuses were also used by hotels to collect customers from the stations, and in large cities for short-distance public transport, well beyond the advent of the motor-car in the 1890s. Horse transport remained quite important in the provinces until the 1920s.

*A small passenger train in the late nineteenth century. In early trains there was no means of communication between compartments. The murder of a passenger on the North London Railway in 1864 led to demands for corridors, as the victim might have been saved if anyone had realised what was going on. Some companies then made windows between compartments: corridors were not introduced until 1891.*

Rail travel was expensive – in 1875 cheap excursion tickets to London from Dorchester (the journey taking six hours), leaving one week and returning the next, cost £1 return first class and 12 shillings third class: even the third class fare was equivalent to a week's wages for a labourer.

The second great advance in transport during the nineteenth century was the bicycle. Early 'bone-shakers' of the 1860s, and 'ordinaries' or penny-farthings of the 1870s and 1880s were difficult to ride, and were mostly used by young men. The introduction of the 'safety' bicycle (looking like a modern machine) in the early 1880s made it possible for the less daring to use bicycles. With the advance from uncomfortable solid tyres to pneumatic ones in the early 1890s the transformation to a modern bicycle was complete, and in 1895-7 cycling was the very highest fashion: there were even aristocratic bicyclists in Hyde Park.

The Hardys were soon caught up by this London fad. Emma took up cycling in 1895, 'doing it rather well' according to Hardy, who wrote in a letter of January 1896: 'I have almost forgotten there is such a pursuit as literature in the arduous study of – bicycling! – which my wife is making me learn to keep her company.' During the spring of 1896, when he was fifty-six, he bought himself a Rover Cob for twenty pounds. In October he was cycling around Dorset with Kipling, who thought the bike rather heavy. Hardy wrote, 'I find it light enough, and am gradually getting to climb a fairly steep hill with it.' He became an enthusiastic cyclist, making

*The omnibus outside the White Hart Hotel, Beaminster, about 1885. This 'bus left Beaminster daily at 10.30 a.m., arriving at Crewkerne seven miles away at 11.35, returning to Beaminster in the afternoon.*

many day trips of forty to fifty miles, and cycling short distances until 1923, when he was eighty-two.

Many women took up cycling in the later 1890s, and not at all always with their staider elders' approval. They (quite correctly) sensed that even more shocking emancipations waited behind this new mobility for the sex. It is said that Emma Hardy was the first woman bicyclist seen in Dorchester. Her green-painted bicycle and matching green velvet dress were made fun of by local contemporaries, and other writers since, but matching clothes and bicycles were then the height of fashion in London. 'Each morning about 7.45 a.m. she would cycle down High West Street (in Dorchester). Her cycle had a foot-rest on the front forks and to see her in her long velvet dress ("pavement-sweepers" we used to call them), free-wheeling with her feet up on the foot-rest and the pedals flying round and round as she coasted down High West Street, was a remarkable sight.'

Hardy often visited the Reverend T. Perkins (a tricyclist) at Turnworth, some seventeen miles from Max Gate, an ideal cycling distance according to Hardy. In 1899 Hardy and Emma attended the harvest festival at Turnworth, and cycled back by moonlight,

*Thomas Hardy with his Rover Cob outside Turnworth Rectory about 1899.*

arriving home at midnight. In the same year he mentioned in a letter that cycling was 'a delightful escape, of a temporary kind, from the cares which crowd in upon one as one grows older'.

In 1903, writing about a friend who had acquired a car, Hardy wrote 'I fear I shall have to stick to the old bike: for one reason (apart from expense) I get exercise on it, while on a motor one gets chills and tooth-ache.' (All Hardy's references to early cars describe riding *on*, rather than *in*, the vehicle – a reflection of their discomfort.) He was being unfair in calling his bike 'old': less than a year earlier he had 'nearly ruined' himself in buying 'a bran-new, free-wheel bicycle', even though 'no respectable person seems to ride one any longer'.

From 1898 Hermann Lea, Thomas Perkins and Hardy made

*Tilley's cycle shop in Weymouth, advertising Rover bicycles, the make of Hardy's first bike. One of the Tilleys taught both Mr and Mrs Hardy to ride. This photograph of about 1895 shows their brand new Benz Velo: the Tilleys were early motorists and motor salesmen.*

many excursions by bicycle to look for suitable scenes for the postcards that were published in 1904 illustrating Hardy's novels. Hermann Lea was a strong cyclist, sometimes riding the hundred miles from London to Dorset. Although the roads were in bad condition, having been neglected because railways were the dominant form of transport, cyclists could keep up good speeds, and indeed were the fastest thing on the roads until cars appeared.

One of Hermann Lea's favourite jokes, doubtless shared with Hardy, is about cycling. A woman wearing 'rational dress' (i.e. knickerbockers) was cycling to Wareham (pronounced Ware'm). Being lost, she asked a roadman: 'Is this the way to Wareham?' He replied: 'Well, Ma'am, I doan't rightly know, but my missus do wear hers beneath her skirt.'

Thomas Hardy's obituary of the Dorset poet William Barnes (d. 1886) records that even on his death-bed Barnes was trying to replace the word bicycle by 'wheel-saddle'. He tried to replace any new classically-derived words with 'Saxon' ones – referring always to photographs as sun-prints, and perambulators as baby-carts.

Neither cars nor bicycles occur in Hardy's fiction because he had

*John Hunt and Sons of Beaminster,*
*described in the 1907 directory as*
*carriage and motor builders, blacksmiths*
*and saw mills, with a motor wagonette*
*for hire.*

virtually stopped writing prose before they became common, and because almost all his fiction is set in the past. His last novel – *Jude the Obscure* was written in 1895, and the last short stories in 1899. During that year he visited Stonehenge by motor-car, writing in a letter afterwards 'I prefer a bicycle, although going at great speeds on a highway was a novelty.' This seems to have been the first time he travelled by car, although Hermann Lea owned one from about this date, when they were still very uncommon. There were not many cars on the road until after 1918, but even in 1902 Hardy wrote 'the motor-cars are rather a nuisance to humble roadsters like me, one never knowing whether the comers are Hooligan-motorists or responsible drivers.' By 'roadster' Hardy meant 'bicyclist'; the American sense, meaning a tramp, seems not to have reached Dorset till later. In 1900 he was doubtful about the comfort of cars. 'It is a disagreeable way of getting about the country I think, and always gives me the back-ache next day. If railway-carriages jolted one so, how we should exclaim against the companies!'

The car was widely regarded as dangerous. In 1907, the Lyme

Regis Borough Council decided the town needed 'motor-car signs'. One such sign confined speed at a narrow point of the main road through the town to 5 m.p.h. The first car seen in Blandford, about 1895, was part of a travelling circus. It made a noise like a threshing machine, frightening all the horses – another reason why cars were disliked.

By 1912 cars were becoming more usual, and Hardy wrote 'Those huge fashionable structures come to our door sometimes and fill us with awe as they superciliously encounter the difficulties of our narrow drive.' By this time either he had changed his mind about the discomfort of cars, or cars had become more comfortable, as he started hiring a car and driver from Tilley's Garage, Dorchester for pleasure trips. During 1912-14 and 1919-27 Harold Voss was his regular driver (in a dark blue Benz), making two trips a week in the summer around the lanes of Dorset. These expeditions were taken at slow speed, never above 25 m.p.h., with many stops to look at the buildings and landscape. The Benz tourer had a hood which could be drawn over for protection, but Voss recalled that Hardy never minded a little rain.

*Harold Voss by the Benz in which he drove Thomas Hardy regularly between 1912 and 1914, and 1919 and 1927 when this photograph was taken outside Talbothayes, the home of Henry, Mary and Kate Hardy.*

From 1914 to 1916 Hermann Lea took Hardy motoring, mostly in west or north Dorset, and occasionally further afield. Hardy never bought a car or learnt to drive. Henry Hardy learnt when he was seventy-three in 1924, but drove too fast in his Sunbeam Talbot tourer to suit his sedate older brother.

Even after the railways had made most of the coach services redundant there was still a huge variety of horse-drawn transport, the main means of travel for shorter distances. In *The Woodlanders* Mrs Charamond's elegant brougham, driven by her coachman, almost collides with Melbury's heavy timber carriage. These vehicles represent two extremes of the scale of vehicles on the road: smart carriages for personal transport and heavy goods transporters.

There were many different types of carriages for the rich to choose from, and having one's own carriage, rather than hiring one or travelling by some form of public transport, was an indication of high social status. In the same novel Melbury promises Grace, his daughter, that if she will marry well 'and keep a stylish carriage', she can then drive past him and not see him 'unless it happened to be in some lonely private place where 'twouldn't lower ye at all'.

Riding provided speedier transport for the single person, and was also regarded as good exercise. In *The Woodlanders*, Fitzpiers borrows his wife's horse in order to visit his mistress easily.

119

*Thomas Hardy's brother Henry in his Sunbeam Talbot in 1923. Henry bought this car and learnt to drive when he was seventy-three.*

Farmers rode about their lands: when Gabriel Oak in *Far from the Madding Crowd* becomes bailiff of two farms he has a 'strong cob', and is seen 'daily trotting in length and breadth of about two thousand acres in a cheerful spirit of surveillance'. In the same novel Bathsheba, like other farmers of the middling sort, has a gig that she drives herself.

Many people who could not afford to keep carriage, coachman, and horses, or who did not need transport daily, hired conveyances when needed. This was true of Hardy himself: although he built a stable and small coach-house at Max Gate this was for the use of visitors. He never owned a carriage or motor-car.

The coming of the railways left many roadside inns bereft of trade. The stage and mail coaches had needed to change horses frequently – often every ten miles. The isolated inns had relied on this trade, supplying travellers with food and changing the horses in a few minutes. Even with the quickest changes of horse coaches could average only ten miles an hour, whereas the earliest of trains could travel at forty. By 1907 the London express to Lyme, in the extreme west of Dorset, was doing the journey in only three hours twenty-six minutes; very little more than the time today.

The Three Tranters (horse carriers) in *Desperate Remedies* was a decayed coaching inn. 'The railway had absorbed the whole stream

*The Acorn Inn, Evershot in the 1890s, which Tess avoided when she passed through the village on her walk to Beaminster to see Angel's parents, breakfasting at a cottage by the church instead. The bicycle by the inn may be Lea's.*

of traffic which formerly flowed by the ancient door of the inn . . . the long line of outbuildings was the most striking and saddening witness to the passed-away fortunes of the Three Tranters. It was the bulk of the original stabling, and where once the hoofs of two-score horses had daily rattled over the stony yard, to and from the coaches without, thick grass now grew.'

For the poorer village people the carrier was the main transport, both for themselves and for goods. Every village either had a carrier based there or one who passed through on his regular trips to the nearest town, usually on market day and Saturday, but sometimes more frequently. Their vans were similar to farmer's wagons, but built slightly less robustly and with narrower wheels because they were used on surfaced roads rather than the land. Most were fitted with canvas covers supported by wooden hoops. In *A Few Crusted Characters*, Hardy describes them as 'a respectable, if somewhat lumbering, class of conveyance, much resorted to by decent travellers not overstocked with money.' They were slow, travelling at not much more than a good walking speed – three or four miles an hour. Mostly they only covered fairly short distances.

In *The Woodlanders* a carrier's van is described as 'rather a moveable attachment of the roadway than an extraneous object' with an old horse 'whose leg-joints, shoulders and hoofs were distorted by harness and drudgery from colthood', having 'trodden this road almost daily for twenty years'. The van 'had a square black tilt [hood] which nodded with the motion of the wheels ... somewhere about the axles was a loose chain, whose only

*George Roberts, baker and grocer of Beaminster, stands at the horse's head, with the rest of his transport fleet drawn up around him. The hand-cart must have served the town, the horse-drawn wagon the outlying customers, and the bicycle deliveries to individual houses.*

known function was to clink as it went.' Mrs Dollery, the driver, wore 'short leggings under her gown for modesty's sake' and a 'felt hat tied down with a handkerchief, to guard against an ear-ache'.

Carriers not only took passengers to and from the market towns, but also carried goods in to be sold and brought purchases back. They also acted as a general delivery service, sometimes even taking back to the village a selection of goods on approval. During the 1920s they changed from horse-drawn vans to motorised coaches or lorries.

The great variety of tasks for which horses were used was reflected in the range of horses bred for specific tasks. The heaviest were farm horses like the Shire. Most were only really suitable for one job, such as carriage work, but market gardeners and small farmers favoured useful 'vanners', who could be put both to field work and pulling a van or wagon. Donkeys were also used for pulling small carts, or loaded with panniers, and for riding. In *The Hand of Ethelberta* the heroine economically rides a donkey from Swanage to Corfe for an archaeological meeting, and has to conceal the fact because it was not a 'proper' way to travel.

*Slade and Sons, carriers from Crewkerne to Beaminster, in about 1898. They brought newspapers from Crewkerne railway station to Beaminster by mid-day.*

The cheapest method of travelling was to walk. Poorer people walked great distances, especially to find work. Tess walked for two days across Dorset so that she could work with her friend Marian. She walked fifteen miles to Angel's parents, and then walked back without seeing them and without her boots.

In *The Mayor of Casterbridge* the hero, Michael Henchard, leaves the town as he entered it twenty-five years before – on foot with his hay-knife and his tool-basket on his back. He walked for five days before looking for work, covering sixteen miles a day. As a child Hardy walked three miles each way to school every day, and it was not unusual for people to walk much longer distances to work daily.

Besides roads and railways there was also sea-transport, although that also suffered when the railways came in. All through the 1830s the Lyme fossil-hunter Mary Anning dispatched her heavier specimens by sea to London; but in 1842 she writes to say she is sending some by 'waggon railroad'. The last regular weekly or fortnightly packets from the Dorset ports to London seem to have finally disappeared in the 1860s. In later years pleasure steamers ran along the Dorset coast in the summer, often with rather grand names, such as the *Empress of India*, *Duke of Devonshire*, *Royal Albert*, *Victoria*, *Lord Roberts*, and so on. Nearly fifty such 'excursioners', almost all paddle-steamers, were registered in Dorset during the century and up to 1914. Before the

*A donkey with loaded panniers going to market. The covered baskets carried by the woman and boy probably contain goods which they are not willing to trust to the donkey, such as eggs.*

*A small cart drawn by a donkey, possibly belonging to a sweep or coalman judging by the grubbiness of the boy leading it.*

*This carriage (a phaeton) was built to carry people, unlike the farm carts and wagons which carried both. The children look rather superior.*

railway reached Swanage in 1885 there were also regular steamers from Swanage to Poole, connecting with the trains to London. Portland stone was taken to London by ship and in *The Well-Beloved* the second Avice makes a trip to the capital in one of the boats. Many other goods, such as coal and timber, travelled by sea, mostly in sailing ships, and trading schooners and small barques remained a common sight up to the First World War.

Dorset has a long and varied coastline, with high cliffs, many bays, and the strange long Chesil ('shingle') Bank enclosing a lagoon and joining the great rock of Portland to the mainland. Since prehistoric times the coast and its ports have been used for defence, fishing and trade; from the middle of the eighteenth century holiday-makers (at first only the rich, and then mainly for medical reasons) visited it as well – early Royal visitors at

*Looking north-west from the top of Portland – a 'singular peninsular once an island and still called such' – along the Chesil Bank – an eighteen-mile 'thin neck of pebbles cast up by ravages of the sea . . . and unparalleled in its kind in Europe.' Portland is the setting for much of* The Well-Beloved. *Weymouth can be seen in the middle distance right, with the hills of the Ridgeway behind.*

Weymouth, and later the hordes brought by the railways for day trips.

The Royal Navy at Weymouth (and later Portland) and the commercial ports of Lyme, Swanage and Poole meant that there were always sailors about in Dorset. Some were on leave from their ships, some half-pay officers, others retired, like the bluff Captain Vye in *The Return of the Native*. He was 'bowed in the shoulders, and faded in general aspect. He wore a glazed hat, ancient boat-cloak, and shoes; his brass buttons bearing an anchor on their face.' When his domestic supply of rum ran out he went to the local inn, and 'standing with his back to the fire, grog in hand, tells remarkable stories of how he lived seven years under the water-line of his ship, and other naval wonders, to the natives, who hoped too earnestly for a treat of ale from the teller to exhibit any doubts of his truth.'

*Looking across Poole quay about 1890: it is very little changed from the photograph of 1850.*

In the eighteenth century the English had no love of the army or soldiers in general, but great respect for the 'Walls of Old England' – their navy and its men. But this attitude to the army markedly changed after the end of the Napoleonic Wars, and was helped on by the growth of the various volunteer branches of the military. In the little valley of Upper Bockhampton, where Hardy was born, there were several such retired naval and military people, which caused it to be nicknamed Veterans' Alley. Hardy must have met many other sea-farers in Dorchester, and in Weymouth and Swanage, where he lived for short periods.

Elizabeth-Jane's real father in *The Mayor of Casterbridge* is a hearty, straightforward sailor, much concerned about the 'drinkables' for her wedding, thinking 'maybe a dozen jars [of rum] will be sufficient, as many of the folk will be ladies, and perhaps they won't drink hard enough to make a high average in the reckoning? . . . I've provided for men and shipmates times enough, but I'm as ignorant as a child how many glasses of grog a woman, that's not a drinking woman, is expected to consume at these ceremonies.' He couldn't stay in 'Casterbridge'/Dorchester, but 'was discovered disconsolately climbing a hill, in his craving to get a glimpse of the sea . . . The contiguity of salt water proved to be such a necessity of his existence' that he preferred to live in 'Budmouth'/Weymouth.

128

*Sailing ships at Poole about 1850 – the sails are spread to dry. From the late sixteenth century Poole was sending ships to Newfoundland, whose crews caught, dried and salted fish there, returning to the Mediterranean to sell them, and finally returning to Poole with a cargo of wine, dried fruits or other Mediterranean produce. Shadrach Joliffe in Hardy's short story* To Please his Wife *takes part in this trade. After about 1850 it ceased to be profitable, and most of the ships of Poole were used for coastal trading.*

Hardy's only sailor hero is the charming if fickle Bob Loveday in *The Trumpet Major*, whose conversation is sprinkled with nautical expressions: 'I merely just for the moment admired you as a sweet little craft . . . Ought I to convoy you home?' He had been in the merchant navy, but joined the Royal Navy, serving on the *Victory* with Captain Hardy at Trafalgar, when the ship 'was near knocked to pieces'.

George III stayed in Weymouth for part of the summer almost every year from 1789 to 1811, turning the commercial port into a fashionable resort. Bob Loveday tells his betrothed "Twould be nothing if it wasn't for the Royal Family, and the lords and ladies, and the regiments of soldiers, and the frigates, and the King's messengers, and the actors and actresses.' Luckily for Weymouth King George continued to stay there, despite the threat of Napoleon invading England by landing on the south coast, and possibly in Dorset. One of Hardy's short stories, *A Tradition of Eighteen Hundred and Four*, shows Napoleon himself landing secretly at Lulworth Cove one night to spy out the land. This was an invention of Hardy's, and he was amused to have it repeated back to him, after publication, as a tradition.

129

The poem 'At Lulworth Cove a century back' commemorates a real visitor to the cove – the poet John Keats on his way to Rome, where he died.

> Had I but lived a hundred years ago
> I might have gone, as I have gone this year,
> By Warmwell Cross on to a Cove I know,
> And Time have placed his finger on me there:

Up to about 1830 visitors came to the coast for medicinal bathing, in the same way that they visited inland spas. In some cases they even drank sea-water. Bathing machines like sheds on wheels were drawn by horse into the deeper water, and immersion was carefully timed and supervised by bathing attendants. Bathing remained segregated until late in the nineteenth century,

*Lulworth Cove, the 'small basin of the sea enclosed by cliffs', where Troy swims and is thought to have been drowned, in* Far from the Madding Crowd. *Cytherea, her brother, and Edward Springrove take 'a very popular local excursion by steamboat' from Weymouth to Lulworth in* Desperate Remedies. *Paddle steamers continued plying along the Dorset coast, and visiting Lulworth, into the 1950s.*

*The photographs were taken in the 1890s, when fishermen still outnumbered tourists. The lobster pots are no longer made of Dorset or Somerset withies (flexible willow branches), but iron or even plastic.*

and some bathing machines remained in use until around 1900. In Lyme men were forbidden to row near the machines into the 1880s. In 1873 the Rev. Francis Kilvert complained 'One has to adopt the detestable custom of bathing in drawers. If ladies don't like to see naked men, why don't they keep from sight?'

Although George III's son, the Prince Regent, preferred Brighton to Weymouth, *The Return of the Native*, set in the 1840s, shows that Weymouth then 'retained sufficient afterglow from its Georgian gaiety and prestige to lend it an absorbing attractiveness to the romantic and imaginative soul of a lonely dweller inland'. Diggory Venn tries to tempt Eustacia Vye with the town: ' "A wonderful place – wonderful – a great salt sheening sea bending up into the land like a bow – thousands of gentlepeople walking up and down – bands of music playing – officers by the sea and officers by land walking amongst the rest – out of every ten folk you meet nine of 'em in love".' Eustacia knows Weymouth, and already has

*Seine fishing either at Lyme Regis or from the Chesil Bank in the 1890s. The fishermen have rowed their boat around a shoal of fish, probably mackerel, close to the shore, and are now pulling in the net. The boat looks like a Portland lerret.*

'romantic recollections of sunny afternoons on an esplanade, with military bands, officers and gallants around.'

Bournemouth, Hardy's Sandbourne, was of much more recent growth. A health resort on a virgin site, developing from the 1830s, it was so select that it tried to stop the vulgar railway coming to the town. A resident wrote:

'But let not Bournemouth, health's approved abode
Court the near presence of the iron road'.

Court it or not, one railway line came in 1870, and another in 1874, and with them a flood of visitors and the lodging houses they needed. The population grew from 691 in 1851 to 16,800 in 1881 and 78,700 in 1911. In *Tess* it is described as 'a fairy place suddenly created by a stroke of a wand, and allowed to get a little dusty . . . a

*Fishermen on the empty coast at Ringstead Bay with White Nothe cliffs behind, where the heroine of* The Distracted Preacher *lights a furze bonfire to warn the smuggling ship that it is unsafe to land.*

glittering novelty'. Tess finally lives with Alec in 'a stylish lodging house' in Bournemouth.

Swanage's growth as a holiday town was not so spectacular as that of Weymouth or Bournemouth. It was a small port where 'everybody in that parish who was not a boatman was a quarrier . . . some wives of the village had learned to let lodgings, and others to keep shops.' Hardy and his first wife Emma stayed in Swanage for some months while he was writing *The Hand of Ethelberta*, finding lodgings 'at the house of an invalided captain of smacks and ketches', who told them smuggling stories. The landlord in the novel is probably based on him. 'The house was so small that the sailor's rich voice, developed by shouting in high winds during a twenty years' experience in the coasting trade, could be heard coming from the kitchen', where 'he slipped about . . . as lightly as a girl and spoke of himself as cook's mate'. When Ethelberta becomes engaged to a peer she and her sister leave the cheerful lodging-house and move to a 'brilliant variegated and stone villa' in Swanage, 'in keeping with their ascending fortunes'.

Smuggling had been important in Dorset, and was tacitly approved by most people, even the gentry. Hardy's grandfather had stored up to eighty tubs (each containing four gallons) of smuggled brandy in the cottage where Hardy was born, making the whole house smell of spirits. In his mother's time an apparently very large woman would appear, asking if 'any of it were wanted cheap'. She carried smuggled spirits in bladders under her clothes. In Lyme wise people stayed indoors when the phrase 'a white hare or rabbit's about' was used – it meant a cargo of smuggled spirits had arrived, and it was best not to notice.

The short story *The Distracted Preacher* shows smuggling as a happy village industry with everyone collecting the tubs of spirits from the smuggling ship, or recovering them from the sea after the ship has left them strung to a rope and sunk with weights. The preacher hero finds that the woman he has fallen in love with is part of a smuggling gang. He is rather a prig, and seems more shocked to find that she acts independently and wears men's clothes while smuggling, than to discover she is breaking the law. She claims in defence that 'My father did it, and so did my grandfather, and almost everyone in Nether-Moynton [Ower-moigne] lives by it, and life would be so dull if it wasn't for that.' Even the earnest clergyman's public preaching fails to convert her, but when Excise officers are offered a reward for any smugglers they catch, either dead or alive, the village gives up the pursuit. She marries the preacher, and is tamed.

The Rev. S. G. Osborne seriously suggested in 1849 that 'smuggling gave a very large amount of employment to the peasantry of this county, and, directly and indirectly, put a great deal of money in their way', and that its suppression was one of the causes of the poverty of the labourer in the nineteenth century.

During the nineteenth century much of the coast was empty, apart from the occasional fisherman, well-to-do visitor or (early in the century) smuggler, although the sea was full of small ships. The photographs reflect this emptiness.

# The Town

*West Walks, Dorchester, one of the double avenues of trees, 'the ancient defences of the town planted as a promenade', which enclosed the town until it grew suburbs in the later nineteenth century.*

*These early photographs of Dorchester were taken about 1860, exactly the date of* The Mayor of Casterbridge, *showing the Dorchester Hardy knew as a young man.*

Hardy was so thoroughly a countryman, and so thought of as a country writer, that people were always surprised to find that he had lived in the centre of London for five years when he was a young man, and for a further three in its southern suburbs. He also lived for short periods in Weymouth, Swanage, and Sturminster Newton in Dorset, and Yeovil in Somerset. But the most important town for him was Dorchester, where he went to school, started work, and lived for 45 years from 1883 until his death. In 1910 he was given the freedom of the Borough of Dorchester, and in his speech of thanks he confessed 'that the freedom of the Borough of Dorchester did seem to me at first something that I had possessed a long while, had helped myself to (to speak plainly), for when I consider the liberties I have taken with its ancient walls, streets, and precincts through the medium of the printing press, I feel that I have treated its external features with the hand of freedom indeed.' He also complained that 'of the shops as I first recollect them [half a century before] not a single owner remains; only in two or three instances does even the name remain . . . Nothing is permanent but change . . . We have become almost a London suburb owing to the quickened locomotion.'

Casterbridge, as Hardy calls his version of Dorchester, is the main setting for one novel, part of the setting of six more, as also of at least ten short stories, and many poems. Along with Bockhampton it is the heart of Hardy's Wessex.

The narrative of *The Mayor of Casterbridge* takes place in the 1850s, a time when Hardy was at school or working in the town. This is before its late nineteenth century expansion, but after the agricultural depression of the 1820s and 1830s had driven many unemployed labourers into the town. Throughout the novel Hardy emphasises the way the town is bound up with the countryside.

Dorchester was 'but the pole, focus, or nerve-knot of the surrounding country life; differing from the many manufacturing towns which are as foreign bodies set down . . . in a green world with which they have nothing in common. Casterbridge lived by agriculture at one remove further from the fountain-head than the adjoining villages – no more.' 'The agricultural and pastoral character of the people upon whom the town depended was shown

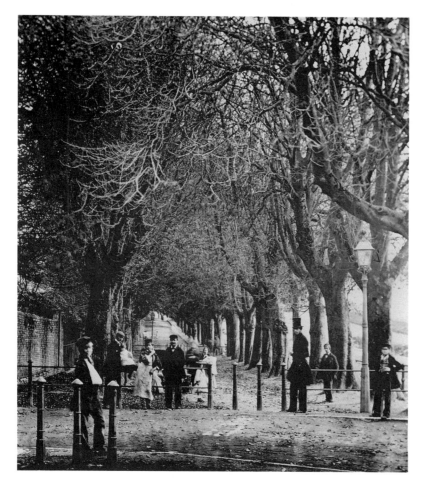

by the class of objects displayed in the shop windows. Scythes, reap-hooks, sheep-shears, bill-hooks, spades, mattocks, and hoes at the ironmonger's . . . ' The most important event was the weekly market. First came the farmers to trade and shop, and then 'field labourers and their wives and children trooped in from the villages for their weekly shopping . . . and pence were handled now as pounds had been handled earlier in the day.' The shops were open until eight o'clock at night, and it was often possible for the labourers to pick up a bargain late on Saturday of fresh goods like meat, which would not keep until Monday.

136

*A travelling knife-grinder with customers and audience, 1880s.*

*Above right:*
*High West Street, Dorchester about 1860.*
*In* The Mayor of Casterbridge *Hardy wrote 'The old-fashioned fronts of these houses, which had older than old-fashioned backs, rose sheer from the pavement, into which bow-windows protruded like bastions.' This was probably the street he had in mind.*

The quarter sessions and assize courts forced many country people to come to Dorchester. The quarter sessions were for lesser offences and were tried by justices of the peace, usually country gentry, although Hardy himself became one. The assize courts were for serious offences, held when the judges came on their circuit, usually only twice a year. The boy who observed the rick-burning in *The Withered Arm* was tried at the assizes, and besides his parents and all the witnesses needed for the trial, Gertrude Lodge made the journey to Dorchester to attempt to cure her withered arm.

The borough magistrates dealt with lesser offences committed within the town: it was at this court in *The Mayor of Casterbridge* that the furmity woman (who sold furmity, a kind of spiced wheat porridge), accused of 'wambling [rolling] about quite dangerous' in the streets, and insulting the constable, reveals to the astonishment of the court, and indeed the whole town, that Henchard had sold his wife twenty years before.

The streets of Dorchester at this period were noisy, lively places, if rather smelly because of bad drains and horses. There were many street musicians as well as market stalls, knife-grinders, and the rest, and Hardy recalled seeing four girls, itinerant musicians, in the main street. In the daytime they seemed commonplace, but in the evening by gaslight 'they were now sublimed to a wondrous charm'. He commemorated them in 'Music in a snowy street'.

*Beaminster market. Hardy describes the similar Dorchester street market in* The Mayor of Casterbridge, *and the difficulties produced by the Dorchester 'tradition that to drive stock it was indispensable that hideous cries, coupled with Yahoo antics and gestures, should be used, large sticks flourished, stray dogs called in . . . all those horned beasts sent women and children to shelter' (often in the hall or passage of the town houses).*

> The weather is sharp
> But the girls are unmoved:
> One wakes from a harp,
> The next from a viol,
> A strain that I loved
> When life was no trial . . .

*Pedlars, like fairs, were losing business in the later nineteenth century because travelling was becoming easier and shops more common.*

*Above right:*
*Alfred Pine's grocery and wine and spirit shop in Beaminster about 1910. It is surprising that so many smart assistants could be needed by such a small shop, but perhaps one or two of the boys were apprentices. Mr Pine can just be seen inside the right-hand window.*

When Elizabeth-Jane sees Dorchester for the first time in *The Mayor of Casterbridge*, from a hill to the east, she declares 'It is huddled all together; and it is shut in by a square wall of trees, like a plot of garden ground in a box edging.' She and her mother stay at the Three Mariners, an ancient inn whose destruction Hardy regretted, but which was 'far from spacious, despite the fair area of ground it covered. The room demanded by intrusive beams and rafters, partitions, passages, staircases, disused ovens, settles, and four-posters, left comparatively small quarters for human beings'. Here they meet some of the inhabitants telling Farfrae that ' "Casterbridge is an old, hoary place o' wickedness, by all account. 'Tis recorded in history that we rebelled against the King one or two hundred years ago, in the time of the Romans, and that lots of us was hanged on Gallows Hill".'

Hardy was interested in the Roman town of Dorchester (Durnovaria), and visited all archaeological excavations in the town. Dorchester 'looked Roman, bespoke the art of Rome, concealed dead men of Rome. It was impossible to dig more than a foot or two deep . . . without coming upon some tall soldier or other of the

empire . . . He was mostly found lying on his side, in an oval scoop
in the chalk, like a chicken in its shell; his knees drawn up to his
chest.' Three graves of this type were found during the building of
Max Gate, and in reporting them in a lecture to the Dorset Natural
History and Antiquarian Field Club, Hardy characteristically
wanted to know about the people of the Roman town and the town's
appearance: 'What social character had the streets, what were the
customary noises . . . did [passengers on the road] ever form a busy
throng such as we now see on a market day?'

   Although Dorchester was so small – only 6,500 inhabitants at
the 1851 census, with half of them living in the surrounding rural
parish of Fordington, it performed all the urban functions. There
were banks, the county courts, a great variety of shops, a prison, a
market, a hospital, a museum, and a workhouse. But it was
physically and economically very close to the land. 'The farmer's
boy could sit under his barley-mow [stack] and pitch a stone into
the office-window of the town-clerk; reapers at work among the

sheaves nodded to acquaintances standing on the pavement corner; the red-robed judge, when he condemned a sheep-stealer, pronounced sentence to the tune of Baa, that floated in at the window from the remainder of the flock browsing hard by; and at executions the waiting crowd stood in a meadow immediately before the drop'.

A few nobility and gentry still kept town houses in Dorchester in the later nineteenth century, and there was a large and varied middle class of professional people and tradesmen; but there was also a large number of the poor. Many of these lived in Fordington, which had originally been a purely agricultural village adjacent to the town. 'Here wheat-ricks overhung the old Roman street, and thrust their eaves against the church tower . . . Barns indeed were so numerous as to alternate with every half-dozen houses . . . Here lived burgesses who daily walked the fallow; shepherds in an intra-mural squeeze.' Lower Fordington, however, around the river, had become an overcrowded urban slum, and the worst part, 'Mixen Lane'/Mill Street 'was the hiding-place of those who were in distress, in debt, and trouble of every kind. Farm-labourers and other peasants, who combined a little poaching with their farming, and a little brawling and bibbing with their poaching, found themselves sooner or later in Mixen Lane. Rural mechanics too idle to mechanize, rural servants too rebellious to serve, drifted or were forced into Mixen Lane.' 'Yet amid so much that was bad, needy respectability also found a home, due to the iron hand of necessity . . . Families from decayed villages – families of that once bulky, but now nearly extinct, section of village society called 'liviers' or lifeholders, whose roof-trees had fallen for some reason or other, came here, unless they chose to lie under a hedge by the wayside.'

Fordington was also the home of a family that was very important to Hardy – the Reverend Henry Moule, vicar of Fordington from 1828-1880, his wife and their seven sons. When he first arrived Moule was disliked by his poorer parishioners because he abolished the church band, and tried to reform everyone's morals, getting the Dorchester horse races stopped in 1833. He also offended the gentry because they thought him Methodist, or too low church. But after he had nursed the parish through the terrible outbreak of cholera in 1854 (caused by the washerwomen of Fordington taking in infected washing from prisoners in Dorchester Barracks) he was a hero to all. His devotion during the epidemic is recorded in Hardy's short story *A Changed Man*.

Moule also wrote to Prince Albert, as guardian of the Duchy of Cornwall, who owned most of Fordington, to try to get him to improve the housing and to release more land for building.

*Mill Street, Fordington, the Mixen Lane* of The Mayor of Casterbridge. *In the middle and late nineteenth century the population density in Fordington was as high as in industrial towns like Manchester, and conditions were even worse than in the agricultural villages. 'Much that was sad, much that was low, some things that were baneful, could be seen in Mixen Lane. Vice ran freely in and out of certain doors of the neighbourhood.'*

*The Reverend Henry Moule and his wife (seated) in front of Fordington Vicarage with their family on August 5th, 1869. Henry the museum curator is standing third from the left, Handley sixth from the left and Horace is standing beside his mother. When Henry Moule died in 1880 Hardy wrote to Handley, 'Though not topographically a parishioner of your father's I virtually stood in that relation to him, and his home generally during many years of my life, and I always feel precisely as though I had been one.'*

Fordington was enclosed by Duchy land, on which no one could build, thus forcing more and more people into the Mill Street area, which was freehold. When Prince Albert took no notice Moule had the letters published in *The Times*.

One of Moule's sons, Horatio, known as Horace, was a great influence on Hardy, helping him with his studies from about 1860, and becoming Hardy's mentor and friend. Horace Moule committed suicide in 1873, to the horror and grief of his family, and Hardy equally.

The oldest brother, another Henry, was curator of the Dorset County Museum from 1881 until his death in 1904. Hardy remembered meeting him for the first time in the late 1850s. Hardy was 'attempting a sketch from nature in water colours . . . he criticised my performance freely'. They became friends, and remained so for nearly fifty years. After Henry Moule's funeral he wrote a long kind letter to another brother, Arthur, a missionary in China, telling him all the detail of the funeral, and writing 'His friendship with me reaches . . . much further back than that of any person now alive and it was of that staunch, undemonstrative kind

St. James, a suburb at the bottom of Shaftesbury's hill was well supplied with water, whereas Hardy wrote that 'within living memory horse, donkeys, and men have been seen toiling up the winding ways to the top of the steep, laden with tubs and barrels filled from wells beneath the mountain.'

Left:
Sherborne, the Sherton Abbas of The Woodlanders, and the marketplace where Giles Winterborne, encumbered with an apple tree, met Grace Melbury when she returned from school. The little hexagonal building in the foreground was built in the early sixteenth century as part of the cloisters. It was the monks' washing-place,

Top left:
Bridport, west of Dorchester, the setting for the short story Fellow-Townsmen.

*A brass band in the market place at Beaminster, probably in the 1880s. It could be the start of a school, or sunday-school treat, as all the boys are on the right and the girls on the left. The woman sitting in the carriage driven by a smart coachman on the left of the photograph may be Mrs Mary Cox.*

which survives all differences of opinion, all contrasting conduct and all separations.'

Dorchester was a garrison town with two barracks, one for infantry, one for artillery, and while there were fewer soldiers than sailors in the county as a whole, there were enough of the former about, both active and retired, for them to be noticeable.

*Above:*
*Company Sergeant Major Frederick Britton of the Royal Garrison Artillery, instructor of the Dorset Volunteer Artillery at Lyme Regis, 1897-1901. The Lyme company was nearly a hundred strong, and practised four times a week. The gun was for repository drill, lifting the barrel out of its mounting with a gin-crane.*

*The first annual camp of the Dorset Rifle volunteers at Lulworth in 1864. Although the rifle volunteers were not regular army like the dragoons who camp on the downs in* The Trumpet Major, *the camps would have been similar. The review in the novel, attended by King George III was much larger.*

There are many in Hardy's fiction, ranging from Troy 'brilliant in brass and scarlet' from the peacetime army in *Far from the Madding Crowd*, to the trumpet-major John Loveday, who along with many of his fellow-soldiers was 'silenced for ever upon one of the bloody battlefields of Spain' during the Napoleonic wars. Hardy was fascinated by the Napoleonic wars, writing of many of the battles in his epic drama *The Dynasts*; but he was horrified by the First World War, which destroyed his faith in the progress of mankind. In 1917 he wrote 'I might say the Good-God theory having, after some thousands of years of trial, produced the present infamous and disgraceful state of Europe . . . a theory of a Goodless-and-Badless God (as in *The Dynasts*) might perhaps be given a trial with advantage.' After the war, in 1919, he thought that 'people were less pitiless towards their fellow-creatures – human and animal – under the Roman Empire than they are now; so why does not Christianity throw in the sponge and say, I am beaten, and let another religion take its place?'

Hardy could not take a simple imperial or jingoistic attitude to either the Boer or First World Wars. His thoughtfulness and capacity to see both sides, and to see war's futility and horror, were not the popular views at the time. He found it supremely ironic that in the German prisoner of war camp at Dorchester 'Men lie helpless here from wounds: in the hospital a hundred yards off other men, English, lie helpless from wounds – each scene of suffering caused by the other!' Frank George, the distant cousin who Hardy hoped would inherit Max Gate, was killed fighting in 1915.

One of Hardy's most memorable poems was composed during the First World War, but Hardy wrote that it 'contains a feeling that moved me in 1870, during the Franco-Prussian War, when I chanced to be looking at such an agricultural incident in Cornwall . . . Query: where was that sentiment hiding itself during more than forty years?' 'In Time of "The Breaking of Nations" ' was published in 1915.

I
Only a man harrowing clods
   In a slow silent walk
With an old horse that stumbles and nods
   Half asleep as they stalk.

II
Only a thin smoke without flame
    From the heaps of couch-grass;
Yet this will go onward the same
    Though Dynasties pass.

III
Yonder a maid and her wight
    Come whispering by:
War's annals will cloud into night
    Ere their story die.

*A crowd outside the public hall in Beaminster (built in 1902) in 1914. The poster on the left asking for 100,000 volunteers for the army was issued in early September 1914: 175,000 men volunteered in the first week.*

The annual fairs were exciting days out for all classes, although during the nineteenth century their business declined and they also became less respectable. In 1885 Woodbury Fair was described as 'a gala day for rustics'. By the middle of the century most of the week-long medieval fairs had shrunk to a couple of days, and the distinctions between gentlefolks' day, all-folks' day, wholesale day, sheep-fair day and so on were lost. Many West Country fairs were on isolated hill-tops such as Woodbury and Weyhill. They had developed early in the medieval period, and in the early eighteenth century Daniel Defoe described Weyhill as 'the greatest fair for sheep . . . that this nation can show'.

The main business of fairs in the nineteenth century was still the auctioning of sheep, horses and other livestock, but there were also the travelling merchants whose presence made fair day the great annual shopping occasion, and increasingly a funfair also. As rural transport became easier less serious shopping was done at the fairs, and apart from flockmasters, farmers and dealers involved with the auctions, they were regarded by most people as holidays.

In *The Mayor of Casterbridge*, Hardy describes the large fair at Weyhill, Hampshire in about 1832, with its 'standing places and pens where many hundreds of horses and sheep had been exhibited and sold' and the 'frivolous contingent of visitors', who 'found a congenial field among the peep shows, toy-stands, waxworks, inspired monsters, disinterested medical men who travelled for the public good, thimble-riggers, nick-nack vendors, and readers of Fate'. The hero, Michael Henchard, sold his wife at the fair, and when she returns some eighteen years later she finds that the funfair has much increased, while 'the real business of the fair had considerably dwindled. The new periodical markets of neighbouring towns were beginning to interfere seriously with the trade carried on here for centuries. The pens for sheep, the tip ropes for horses, were about half as long as they had been. The stalls of tailors, hosiers, coopers, linen-drapers, and other such trades had almost disappeared, and the vehicles were far less numerous.'

Fairs involved much drinking, and were regarded as rather wicked. They brought some of the worst of the town into the

*Lea recorded that when he visited the fair to take the photographs, winkles could be bought for a penny a plate, including pepper and vinegar.*

countryside. The very bashful Joseph Poorgrass in *Far from the Madding Crowd* was sent to Greenhill fair 'where there were womenfolk riding round – standing on horses with hardly anything on but their smocks', but even that failed to cure him.

In 1873 Hardy walked the thirteen miles east from Dorchester to Woodbury fair, the original of Greenhill fair in *Far from the Madding Crowd*, which he was then writing. The local paper report for the fair that year says that 'the morning was very fine, and the air bracing', but 'in the pleasure part of the fair there was a great falling off in attendance . . . Much amusement was caused by the "Steam wheels of life"; these were well patronised from sturdy youth up to the venerable white-haired patriarch of seventy years. The whole proceeding passed off with considerable quietness.' This is transformed in the novel, set at twenty years earlier, to 'the busiest, merriest, and noisiest day of the whole statute number was the day of the sheep fair. At the fair, Bathsheba, the heroine,

*The galloping horses or roundabout at Woodbury Hill Fair about 1900. Lea wrote 'old and young, rich and poor, male and female, delight to ride in deafening proximity to the organ, which from time to time loses its head completely . . . and gives vent to quaint howls and shrieks of protracted agony.'*

*Wagons and flocks of sheep going up to Woodbury Hill fair. This was the Greenhill fair of* Far from the Madding Crowd. *Lea showed Hardy all these photographs of the fair in 1901, and Hardy wrote to Lea to say that they were excellent.*

watches a splendid melodramatic performance of 'Dick Turpin's Ride to York and the Death of Black Bess', without realising that the hero is her errant husband Troy.

A charming but unlikely story is told of the origin of Woodbury fair. A packman whose goods had been soaked by rain spread them out on Woodbury Hill to dry. Local people, seeing them, came and bought. As the trade was so good he returned the next year, and so the fair grew up. Medieval fairs were in fact carefully controlled, and Woodbury had a royal charter from 1232. The tolls from the fairs were very profitable to those granted charters. Hutchins, the county historian, says that before 1730 the profit was over £100 a

Auctioneer at Woodbury Hill fair, about 1900.

Top left:
Bradley, hatter, hosier, tailor and outfitter from Wareham with heaps of clothes for sale, spread on cloths on the ground.

Left:
It is possible that the heap carefully placed on the large cloth is watercress, but if so they are expecting to sell a huge quantity.

*Part of the horse sale at Woodbury Fair about 1900. The imaginative eloquence of the horse dealers at this date was much admired – 'Look how he steps. Just like a member of Parlyament.'*

year, but after that it declined to £30 or £40. During the 1890s, 2,000 sheep were sold annually at the fair, and 60 to 80 horses, but after the First World War it shrank considerably and was stopped during the Second. An attempted revival in 1948 was ruined by heavy rain, and it has not been held since.

Hermann Lea visited Woodbury fair around 1900 to take the photographs seen here, and described the 'penny peep-show, containing pictures of the most horrible and atrocious crimes on record'. Especially popular was one of a house on fire 'with a lady, in scant attire, gracefully diving from a top window, with the apparent intention of impaling herself on some spiked railings.' The showman monotonously intoned ' "Observe the flames, the cruel flames a-reaching hout to try and wrap 'er in their cruel embrace, observe the gallant fireman a-'urrying round the corner to the bloody scene and all in vain, 'cos 'e's too late".'

Towns also had their fairs and markets, and these increased their business at the expense of the rural fairs after the railways were built, as it was easier to get animals to a market town than to a remote hillside. Hiring fairs, like the one Gabriel Oak attends in Dorchester were usually held in towns. In *Far from the Madding Crowd* Gabriel stood with 'two to three hundred blithe and hearty labourers waiting upon chance . . . Among these, carters and waggoners were distinguished by having a piece of whip-cord twisted round their hats; thatchers wore a fragment of woven straw; shepherds held their sheep-crooks in their hands; and thus the situation required was known to the hirers at a glance.' The Dorchester hiring fair was at Old Candlemas Day (February 14th) and agreements were made there between the labourers and farmers for a year's work from old style Lady Day, April 6th.

# Farming the Land

The term farmer covered a wide variety of people in the nineteenth century, ranging from gentlemen farmers who owned their land and employed stewards or bailiffs to run their farms and estates, to peasant farmers with small farms that they ran single-handed and who might be very nearly as poor as the labourers they could not afford to employ. Many of these very small farmers were also part-time, like Wildeve in *The Return of the Native*. He keeps an inn (The Quiet Woman, whose sign 'represented the figure of a matron carrying her head under her arm') as well as farming reclaimed heathland.

The 1868 Commission on the Employment of Children and Women in Agriculture selected a typical farm of 660 acres in Dorset, and gave a list of the labourers employed. The farm had 500 acres of arable, 120 acres of pasture, and 40 acres of downland, and employed 29 men and boys all through the year, with four extra men and eleven extra women for harvest. The farm was surveyed during a boom in farming, and before much mechanisation (apart from in threshing) had taken place, so that the numbers employed were high, and typical – three men and two boys per 100 acres was the average in the early to mid nineteenth century. Four carters and four carter-boys looked after the horses that provided all the transport and part of the power for the farm. Human strength supplied the rest. Two shepherds, a shepherd-boy, a cow-man and a cow-boy looked after the other livestock. Twelve ordinary labourers and four plough-boys did the rest of the work. Employing all these people for a full year cost the farmer £788. The farm Bathsheba took over in *Far from the Madding Crowd* was similar to this one.

In 1815 half the land in Dorset was let to tenant farmers; the other half was split between the farms the big land-owners kept in their own hands, and those owned freehold by smaller farmers. Many farm leases had been for life, or even for a series of lives (copyhold), but after the later eighteenth century shorter terms became common, because the land-owners wanted more control over their tenants. Farming was becoming more business-like. By 1850 yearly leases were common, and changes of tenant frequent.

In 1848 Waterston Farm, near Puddletown, the model for

Bathsheba's house in *Far from the Madding Crowd*, had been held for fifty years by the same tenant, father and son, but this was pointed out as an exception. Often tenants moved on to bigger or better farms, but some were unable to pay their rent and were evicted. Bathsheba fears this will happen after Troy has neglected the farm; 'in the event of her inability to meet the agent at the forthcoming January rent-day very little consideration would be shown . . . once out of the farm the approach of poverty would be sure'. (Bathsheba's tenancy of her farm is an odd combination of yearly tenancy, and, since her uncle was able virtually to leave her the farm, the medieval copyhold.) Hardy chronicles several families, such as the Durbeyfields, who had once been large land-owners, but who are fallen to being labourers; even in the nineteenth century failed farmers had to accept this fate, or join the drift to the towns.

There were a few women farmers like Bathsheba in *Far from the*

*Haymaking at Combe Down Farm, Beaminster in 1912 Mr Dawbeny, wearing white clothes, stands in the centre of his men, looking as if he belongs to a different world. The stoneware cider jar in its wicker cradle is being plied.*

156

*Mowing with a scythe. Attached to his belt is a whetstone for sharpening the scythe, which had to be done frequently.*

*Above right*
*Tory's Barton, Turnworth, in the 1890s. The novelist Rider Haggard visited Mr Tory in 1902, describing him as a 'gentleman who belongs to the old school of yeoman farmers, of whom he is a perfect type.' At that time Mr Tory 'believed the outlook to be as bad as possible' for agriculture. He and his brother farmed 6,000 acres: he bred Dorset Down sheep and kept his own strain of barley seed. The half barrels probably contain cattle food, and the wagon is either loaded with hay for the cows to eat or straw for their bedding. The building (background right) is a granary, set up on staddle-stones to keep out rats and other vermin.*

*Madding Crowd.* Hardy must have heard of Mrs Catherine Hawkins, a young widow in East Dorset who ran a farm of 525 acres with the help of a bailiff, because his cousin Tryphena Sparks worked as a pupil teacher in the same area.

William Barnes, the Dorset poet, said that 'in a great gathering of labourers and farmers at a fair' he could distinguish the young farmers because they were 'in the main, finer and more shapely men, and men of better bodily carriage'; whereas the young labourers were 'very ungainly, if not stunted'. He thought that this was due not only to the poor food of the labourers, but also because they were set to hard work when they were too young. Farmer's children were more likely to stay on at school, while nineteenth-century farmers were less likely to work in the fields alongside their men, as they had done earlier, except possibly at harvest.

Mechanisation was reducing the number of men employed, and an entirely new breed – the engineer – was appearing on farms. In *Tess* the engineer who brings the threshing machine is described as 'in the agricultural world, but not of it. He served fire and smoke; these denizens of the fields served vegetation, weather, frost and sun . . . The long strap which ran from the driving wheel

157

of his engine to the red thresher under the rick was the sole tie-line between agriculture and him.' The high cost of these new machines, and the only intermittent need for them on individual farms, combined with rural suspicion of machinery, led to the growth of these external contractors. Their workmen were paid up to thirty shillings a week, two or three times the labourer's wage. A story told in Dorset, but known all over the country, tells of a farmer who said he would be happy with the new steam ploughs and threshers if he had a lake at one end of his field and a mine at the other, since the machine's appetite for both water and coal was large. Eddison's Steam Plough Works in Dorchester, set up in 1870, was a large contracting firm, which survived the agricultural depression of the 1880s by going over to steam-rollers for road work. Hardy and other Fordington residents tried in the 1890s to stop Eddison's loud hooter, which blared out at 5.45 am every morning.

Many more people had been the equivalent of farmers before the medieval open fields had been enclosed. The arable strips had been shared among virtually the whole village, and there was communal grazing for all animals. Most of the good agricultural land had been enclosed by the later eighteenth century, but the fencing of the wastes and commons continued into the next. These had been of great benefit to the labourers, and to the smaller farmers. The commons had been used for grazing, and the commons and waste had both provided fuel.

Hardy lived in Dorchester while Fordington was still being farmed as open fields. Fordington Great Field contained 1,500 acres with no fences until 1874, when the parish was enclosed to make three farms where formerly as many as forty tenants had held land. Enclosure led to much more efficient agriculture: it was impossible to breed stock selectively when all animals were herded together, and small holders of land in open fields could not undertake draining, and other land improvement. But the cost was high for those squeezed out. A large class of landless labourers, whose cottages were owned by the farmers and tied to the job, was created by enclosure, and it became far more difficult for anyone to start in agriculture when there were no commons available for grazing.

Despite these disadvantages, it was still possible in the nineteenth century for the slightly better-off agricultural worker –

*A farmer or a farmer's son with a bull. He is carrying a gun: many farmers enjoyed shooting as much as the landowners. The bull is a Longhorn, which was the commonest type of cattle in Dorset until it was gradually replaced by the Shorthorn during the nineteenth century.*

a stockman or carter – to become a farmer. In *Far from the Madding Crowd* Gabriel Oak, who started as a shepherd like his father, was 'enabled by sustained efforts of industry and chronic good spirits to lease a small sheep farm', which was stocked with sheep by a dealer 'who was receiving a percentage ... until such time as the advance should be cleared off'. When all Gabriel's flock die falling into a chalk-pit, he has to give up; 'the value of his stock, plant, and implements which were really his own' just paid his debts. Farmers did not want to employ him as a bailiff because he had had a farm of his own, so he returns to being a shepherd. He finally obtains a farm by marriage.

Farmers gained many middle-class attributes during the nineteenth century. When his prospects look good, at the beginning of the novel, Gabriel tries to tempt Bathsheba with some of them; 'one of those little ten-pound gigs for market – and nice flowers and birds ... And a frame for cucumbers – like a gentleman and lady'; and, in a year or two, a piano. 'Farmers' wives are getting to have pianos now'.

The game laws, and the passion of the upper classes – even the urban *nouveaux riches* – for hunting, shooting and fishing meant

159

*Shocks or stooks of corn drying in the sun. These are unusually small ones, suggesting that it was a poor crop. For as long as a single sheaf (called a policeman when left deliberately) stood in the fields, the women and children could not enter the field to lease or glean the left-over corn for their own use.*

that well-to-do landlords could preserve all sorts of game, from rabbits and hares to deer (and most importantly the fox) on tenanted land. Farmers had their crops damaged by the wild animals, and by the hunt passing through. Labourers were prosecuted as poachers for taking even rabbits.

Farming has always been dependent on the weather, and the price that produce will fetch, and during the nineteenth century farmers' fortunes fluctuated. Up to 1813 prices were high because the Napoleonic wars made the importing of foodstuff difficult, and because there was a series of bad harvests. The area under cultivation expanded at this time because demand was so great. Doubtless much of the miser Benjamin Derriman's money in *The Trumpet Major* was derived from the large war-time profits in agriculture.

An agricultural depression started even before the end of the war in 1815 (an exceptionally good harvest in 1813 virtually halved the price of corn) and agriculture did not recover for twenty-five years. Farmers' incomes were greatly reduced, and many land-owners had to reduce rents in order to keep tenants, but it was the labourers who suffered the most, since they were closest to the bread-line. From 1837 increasing demand for agricultural produce, stimulated by the general expansion of industry in towns,

160

and combined with increasing productivity due to more scientific methods in draining, fertilizing, and concentrated foodstuffs for livestock, led to a recovery. Farming entered its golden age of development, and farmers' earnings increased. This is the period of *The Mayor of Casterbridge* and *Far from the Madding Crowd*.

Bad harvests in the later 1870s coincided disastrously with the first influx of corn from America and Canada, and precipitated another agricultural depression, which was not to lift until after 1900. Yet since so many other former trades had left Dorset for the north of England, agriculture remained the most important industry there long after it had caused to be so elsewhere. In 1800 agriculture was the largest and most important industry nationally, but by 1900 it was producing only six percent of the national income. Dorset is still today a thinly populated county because of its lack of non-agricultural industry.

Just as the prosperity and status of farmers varied, so did the land they farmed. The poorest was the heathland of eastern Dorset, with a thin acid soil that after clearing needed continual fertilizing to produce crops. The chalk downland was made fertile by large flocks of sheep, and the claylands and river valleys were very productive, with much dairying. Most farms were mixed, producing corn and other crops as well as keeping animals, but some, especially dairy farms, were more specialised.

Corn, particularly wheat and barley, has always been grown in Dorset. In *Far from the Madding Crowd* Gabriel Oak struggles to protect from the storm five wheat-ricks and three stacks of barley 'seven hundred and fifty pounds in the divinest form that money can wear – that of necessary food for man and beast'. The sheep he looked after would have been used as 'walking manure carts' to fertilize the downlands, so that all this corn could be grown. The sheep fed during the day on water-meadows or downland pastures, and then were penned at night on the arable fields, the sheep-fold or pen being moved every night so that the whole field was manured. The ground was ploughed before the sheep were put to it, and after they had manured it seed was sown broadcast – wheat in the autumn or barley in the spring.

This primitive sowing method was not superseded until the 1840s or 1850s, when the seed drill came into general use. The arrival of the first of these machines in Dorchester is described in *The Mayor of Casterbridge*. It 'created about as much sensation in the corn-market as a flying machine would create at Charing Cross . . . it resembled as a whole a compound of hornet, grasshopper, and shrimp, magnified enormously'. Lucetta says 'it is a sort of agricultural piano'. The innovating Farfrae correctly prophesies that 'it will revolutionise sowing hereabout! No more sowers flinging their seed about broadcast, so that some falls by the wayside and some among thorns, and all that. Each grain will go straight to its intended place.'

Often it was women who weeded the wheat and barley 'cutting up thistles and other noxious plants with a spud [a small spade]'. Women were also employed for corn harvest; '. . . a lively time. The bonus in wages during these few weeks, the cleanliness of the occupation, the heat, the cider and ale, influence [the women] to facetiousness and vocal strains.' (*The Dorsetshire Labourer*)

The labourers and their wives depended on the extra wages paid at harvest for overtime or piece work – varying in total from one pound to three pounds each – to buy shoes and clothing, since it was the only time of the year they earned anything approaching a good wage. Extra helpers were seized for the harvest: when there is a bad, late harvest in *The Mayor of Casterbridge* 'nearly the whole town' is out in the fields, working by moonlight.

The corn was first cut by either the short sickle or the larger scythe, depending upon local prejudice as to which was the best tool. Sometimes travelling gangs of mowers (5,000 Irish reapers came to England in the summer of 1855) were employed, or the labourers of the farm would do the cutting. Mechanical reapers, drawn by horses, were used from the 1860s but, as shown in *Tess of the D'Urbervilles*, the machines could not 'open' a field, so 'a lane a few feet wide had been hand-cut through the wheat' around the edge of the field. After cutting the corn was bound into sheaves, and this is Tess's job. 'From the last sheaf finished she draws a handful of ears, patting their tips with her left palm to bring them even. Then stooping low she moves forward, gathering the corn with both hands against her knees, and pushing her left gloved [against thistles] hand under the bundle to meet the right on the other side, holding the corn in an embrace like that of a lover. She

*A donkey cart, loaded with baskets, tools and a single sheaf of corn, probably gleaned. Many poor families leased or gleaned corn, threshed it at home, and took it to the miller to be ground into flour. The miller would take a proportion (usually one sixth) of the flour in payment, and he would sometimes be accused of not returning the flour made from the corn delivered, but inferior stuff.*

162

*Steam threshing tackle at work. The traction engine has drawn into the rickyard, with the threshing machine attached to it by a belt-drive. The man on the skyline is pitching sheaves of corn down from the rick to be threshed; the grain is coming out into the large sacks, the straw at this end of the machine. The straw is being made into a rick in the left foreground.*

brings the end of the bond together, and kneels on the sheaf while she ties it.'

The sheaves are then placed on end, ears up, leaning together, 'till a shock, or "stitch" as it were here called, of ten or a dozen was formed'. These shocks were left to stand in the sun and wind to dry, which in bad weather could be a drawn-out process. There was one terrible harvest on one farm in the late nineteenth century when the last sheaf was not finally brought to the farmyard until Christmas Eve. Mechanical reapers that also bound the corn into sheaves came into use in the 1890s, reducing the amount of labour needed in the harvest field. Given decent weather the harvest would be home by the end of October, far later than today, when quicker-maturing strains of corn are grown and it is no longer dried in the fields.

After being carted back to the farm on wagons, the corn was built into ricks where it completed its drying, protected from the weather by thatch or tarpaulin. The ear had then to be threshed from the straw. In *Tess* the old men making a straw rick beside the steam threshing machine talk 'of the past days when they had been accustomed to thresh with flails on the oaken barn floor; when everything, even the winnowing [separating the grain from the husks and other rubbish] was effected by hand labour, which, to their thinking, though slow, produced better results'. The introduction of horse-driven threshing machines was one of the causes of the agricultural riots of the 1830s, because the labourers saw them as a threat to their main winter job of threshing. When mobile steam-driven machines came in, like the one in *Tess*, all the threshing on a farm could be done in a few days.

Hardy represents the threshing machine as a tyrant, 'keeping up a despotic demand upon the endurance of their muscles and nerves'. The farmer is the real tyrant – he gives Tess the worst job – spreading out all the sheaves as they enter the machine – and will not let anyone take her place for very long. In *The Dorsetshire Labourer* Hardy says 'Not a woman in the county but hates the threshing machine. The dust, the din, the sustained exertion demanded to keep up with the steam tyrant are distasteful to all women but the coarsest.'

*Thatching a corn rick was skilled work: sometimes a rick would need to have wooden props inserted to keep it standing, to the shame of its builders.*

Corn ricks were raised from the ground on brushwood or iron stands to help them drain, and to try to preserve them from rats, but they still got in. When the threshers reached the bottom of the rick rat-hunting would begin. All the best ratters amongst the village dogs would appear, and as many as possible were killed by the labourers and the dogs. Some always escaped to provide more offspring for next year. As a field of corn was cut rabbits would be trapped in the ever-decreasing area of uncut corn, and when the area was tiny, work would stop while these were caught.

Thousands of sheep were kept in Dorset, partly because they were needed to fertilize the arable fields, but also for their meat and wool. Until artificial fertilizers were introduced in the mid-nineteenth century sheep were the sheet-anchor of arable farming in Dorset. The life of a shepherd had changed little since prehistoric times. Like all farming it had an unchanging rhythm through the year, dictated by lambing in late winter or early spring and shearing in early summer. Feeding stuff for sheep improved during the later eighteenth and nineteenth century with the introduction of new crops like clover. All stockmen had to doctor their animals: Gabriel Oak has to rescue sheep which get

*A large flock of sheep grazing not two miles from Dorchester, with the 'stupendous ruin' of Maiden Castle (the huge Iron Age hillfort) in the background. The pasture is broken up with furze bushes. In* A Tryst at an Ancient Earthwork *Hardy wrote that Maiden Castle's profile 'is as cleanly cut as that of a marble inlay. It is varied with protuberances, which . . . have the animal aspect of warts, wens, knuckles, and hips.'*

into a field of young clover and eat so much of it that they 'blast'. He performs the delicate operation of piercing their stomachs. Water-meadows, which were protected from frost by a thin sheet of moving water, had provided spring grazing for sheep from the seventeenth century, producing grass just as the store of winter food ran out. As with much farming, mechanisation in the later nineteenth century made the shepherd's job easier, without essentially altering it. Along with carters and cowmen, shepherds were paid slightly more than general labourers because they took responsibility for animals.

Sheep and shepherds are found in much of Hardy's fiction, and in *Far from the Madding Crowd* are entwined with the plot. At the beginning of the novel Gabriel Oak's flock is lambing, and he is living with them on the downs, in a shepherd's hut like 'a small Noah's Ark' on wheels, 'to shelter the shepherd in his enforced nightly attendance'. Gabriel slept in the hut, 'on a rather hard couch, formed of a few corn sacks'. Lambing was a hard and lonely time for shepherds, with the flock needing attention all the time. Gabriel's earliest overtures to Bathsheba include taking her a motherless lamb 'in a respectable Sunday basket' for her to rear. He later became her shepherd, looking after her 'old Wessex horned' flock. This breed was particularly good for folding on arable ground because they had long strong legs for walking from the water-meadows to the arable fields every day, and were sociable, not minding the close penning in the folds.

165

A shepherd with his dogs, probably in Puddletown in the 1880s. This could be Gabriel Oak with his two dogs – old George who had arrived at 'an age at which all superfluous barking was cynically avoided as a waste of breath'. He only barked at the sheep to order, 'when it was done with an absolutely neutral countenance . . . to frighten the flock for its own good.' The younger dog 'had no name in particular, and answered with perfect readiness to any pleasant interjection' Far from the Madding Crowd.

Washing sheep was done early in the morning so that the sheep would dry out during the day, and not catch cold. In Far from the Madding Crowd *Gabriel* 'stood on the brink' and thrust the sheep under 'as they swam along, with an instrument like a crutch' – just as is happening here.

Dipping sheep at Puddletown about 1895. The sheep are not being washed in the pool, but in a small trough filled with water containing a dip to kill parasites like the blow fly. The sheep have recently been shorn – the ridges left by the shears can be seen clearly. They must be lively sheep to need penning in extra high hurdles. The last to be dipped were the shepherds' dogs – if done first they ran home.

167

*Shearing at Bradford Peverell near Dorchester in 1885. In* Far from the Madding Crowd *the barn doors were thrown open, and 'here the shearers knelt, the sun slanting upon their bleached shirts, tanned arms, and the polished shears they flourished . . . the captive sheep lay panting, quickening its pants as misgiving merged to terror, till it quivered like the hot landscape outside'. The woman is tying up the fleeces.*

At Puddletown Gabriel has no lambing hut, and has to take the sick and orphan lambs to Warren's Malthouse, arriving with 'four lambs hung in various embarrassing attitudes over his shoulder'. New-born lambs have 'four legs large enough for a full-grown sheep, united by a seemingly inconsiderable membrane about half the substance of the legs collectively, which constituted the animal's entire body just at present'. As the malthouse fire revives them, Gabriel feeds the motherless ones milk from a small teapot.

At the end of May sheep are washed in especially constructed pools. 'A tributary of the main stream flowed through the basin of the pool by an inlet and outlet at opposite points.' Gabriel and the others 'were assembled here, all dripping wet to the very roots of their hair . . . The meek sheep were pushed into the pool . . . [and] let out against the stream . . . all impurities flowing away below.' After leaving the sheep for at least a week so that the fleece is clean and dry, shearing takes place. As often happened, Gabriel and the farm labourers were assisted by travelling sheep-shearers. 'They sheared in the great barn, called for the nonce the Shearing-barn, which on ground-plan resembled a church with

*A group of sheep-shearers near Beaminster, in about 1910. Several of them have pairs of shears in their hands, and they have two stoneware jars of beer or cider between them. The man standing on the left was a drover, 'Coo' Denner. He was cross-eyed, and people crossed their fingers when they met him to avert the evil eye.*

transepts. It not only emulated the form of the neighbouring church . . . but vied with it in antiquity.' The shearers used hand-shears, which made it a tough task. Gabriel could shear a sheep in twenty-three and a half minutes, 'gradually running the shears in line after line round her dewlap [throat skin], thence about her flank and back, and finishing over the tail.' (This was the fastest Bathsheba had ever seen.) One of the women then 'throws the loose locks into the middle of the fleece, rolls it up', and then ties it into a bundle with a woollen rope.

When the shearing is finished Bathsheba gives her men a sheep-shearing supper. Hermann Lea attended such a supper at Athelhampton in the 1880s, and testifies to the truth of Hardy's description. Lea recorded that one of the shearers sang a song. 'I tried to keep count of the verses, but after the sixteenth I lost count and became bewildered. Still it went on, and on, until finally the standing singer was forcibly pulled down by his neighbour.' Hardy told Lea that he only described 'such things as he had actually

169

experienced, or learned by actual first-hand knowledge', and since at Athelhampton, Lea was close to Puddletown, where *Far from the Madding Crowd* was set, and only about ten years after it was written, he was possibly seeing the originals of the labourers in the novel.

In September some of the sheep are sold at the local fair. 'Shepherds who attended with their flocks from long distances started from home two or three days, or even a week, before the fair, driving their charges a few miles each day – not more than ten or twelve – and resting them at night in hired fields by the wayside.' Many routes involved the use of the centuries-old drovers' roads, with hedges set back and especially wide verges, where cattle or sheep could browse at any stop. Such roads may

*A flock of sheep being driven through Bere Regis in the 1880s. Before motor transport most animals were driven to market, and then to the butcher. Gabriel would have driven Bathsheba's sheep through Bere Regis on the way to Woodbury Fair.*

170

*A milkmaid wearing a scarf rather than a bonnet so that she can get close to the cows to milk them. 'All the men, and some of the women, when milking, dug their foreheads into the cows and gazed into the pail. But a few – mainly the younger ones – rested their heads sideways' Tess of the D'Urbervilles.*

still be widely seen in Dorset. Being close to the fair Gabriel drives the sheep over on the morning of the fair.

In the last year of his life Hardy 'recalled how, crossing the ewe-leaze when a child, he went down on hands and knees and pretended to eat grass in order to see what the sheep would do. Presently he looked up and found them gathered around in a close ring, gazing at him with astonished faces.'

In *Tess of the D'Urbervilles*, Tess spends her happiest time working for Dairyman Crick, in 'the Valley of the Great Dairies, the valley in which milk and butter grew to rankness'. Tess has lived in the Blackmoor Vale, also a dairying area, but here 'the enclosures numbered fifty acres instead of ten, the farmsteads were more extended, the groups of cattle formed tribes here about; there only families.'

With the expansion of towns, increased population and generally improving prosperity, demand for milk in the towns increased dramatically in the second half of the nineteenth century, and quick transport by rail made its delivery possible. Dairy farming increased in Dorset, as in other areas, which meant that more dairymaids and men were needed, as all milking was by hand until after the First World War. Dairyman Crick sends his milk to London by train, and he speaks sharply to a milker who hasn't washed her hands: ' "Upon my soul, if the London folk only knowed of thee and thy slovenly ways, they'd swaller their milk and butter more mincing than they do a'ready; and that's saying a good deal".' Tess and Angel Clare take the churns filled with milk to the station in the dairyman's cart, and Tess is amused to think of strange people, Londoners, drinking it for their breakfasts – ' "Noble men and noble women, ambassadors and centurions, ladies and tradeswomen, and babies who have never seen a cow".' After 1910 some milk was sterilized or pasteurised, but in the later nineteenth century if the weather became too hot the towns ran short of milk, because it went sour before it could be got there.

The dairymaids' days started early, between three and four in the morning, with the first milking. Yesterday's milk was then skimmed by hand to remove the cream for butter making. The dairyman has a large churn turned by a horse-gin to make butter in. When the cream will not turn to butter 'the dairy was paralysed', and the dairyman fears he will have to consult Conjurer Trendle, a white witch. He displays a common ambiguous attitude to this: 'I have said fifty times, if I have said once, that I don't believe in en. But I shall have to go to 'n if he's·alive. Oh yes, I shall have to go to 'n, if this sort of thing continnys!' Luckily the cream turns, and saves him consulting the person he pretends not to believe in.

Cheese is also made. Tess and Angel break the curds before putting them into vats: 'The operation resembled the act of crumbling bread on a large scale'. They may have been making the Dorset Blue Vinny, one of the less popular local cheeses now no longer produced. It was a very hard, poor cheese with blue veining made from skimmed milk, after the cream had been removed for butter. The labourers ate a good deal of it, and cheese generally formed a major part of their diet.

In the later afternoon the second milking took place. Tess arrived at Talbothays as 'a prolonged and repeated call "Waow! Waow!"' rang out. 'The red and white herd nearest at hand, which had been phlegmatically waiting for the call, now trooped towards the steading . . . their great bags of milk swinging under them as they walked.' After the second milking, and skimming the morning's milk, one presumes the dairy maids and men went to an early bed to start the whole process again the next day.

*Milking in a farmyard at West Stafford in the 1890s. This is in the Valley of the Great Dairies, and may be the prototype for Talbothayes in* Tess of the d'Urbervilles: *'Long thatched sheds stretched round the enclosure, their slopes encrusted with vivid green moss.' The cows 'that would stand still of their own will were milked in the middle of the yard.' A milk churn can be seen beyond the cow being milked. Pigs were often kept on dairy farms as they could be fed on any left-over skimmed milk (the by-product of butter and cream) and the whey from cheese-making.*

Farmers had to put much effort into growing fodder crops to keep their animals through the winter when the grass does not grow. At Flintcomb-Ash farm, 'a starve-acre place', Tess and Marian are set to hacking turnips or swedes. 'The upper half of each turnip has been eaten off by the livestock, and it was the business of the women to grub up the lower or earthy half of the root with a hooked fork called a hacker, that it might be eaten also.' This is a cold, winter-time job, and since they are being paid piece-work rates they continue working even when it rains. 'When it was not swede-grubbing it was swede-trimming, in which process they sliced off the earth and the fibres with a bill-hook before storing

172

*A mower in a hayfield with his scythe and rake, about 1870. Although wages were so low, labourers usually had to provide their own hand tools.*

*Making a hayrick at Abbotsbury on the Dorset coast in the 1890s. The loose hay is being taken to the top of the rick by an elevator driven by a horse-gin. The horse walks round in a circle turning a pair of gears that drive the elevator via a long shaft. Dairyman Crick's large butter churn in* Tess of the D'Urbervilles *was driven by a horse-gin.*

the roots for future use.' Root crops for winter feed were an eighteenth-century introduction.

Much of the hay was made from the water-meadows. After the sheep had grazed them in early spring, the meadows were left to grow, and the grass cut for hay in June. As with the corn harvest, extra people were needed, and anyone who could lent a hand. In *Far from the Madding Crowd*, Troy, on leave from the army, helps

*Making a hayrick at Newtown, Beaminster, about 1900. A large number of people were always required to carry out such operations, in marked contrast with the present. Even so sympathetic an observer as the Reverend S. G. Osborne could describe labourers as forming 'farm machinery in their mass'.*

*A hurdle-maker at Puddletown in the 1880s or 1890s. The uprights for the hurdle are pushed into holes in a long heavy piece of wood set into the ground – a hurdle-maker's only piece of equipment apart from his small sharp bill-hook. His raw material – hazel – is seen behind him, and a pile of finished hurdles to the right; the litter of off-cuts is all around.*

*Mowing hay with a scythe.*

with the hay-making on Bathsheba's farm. He 'had come hay-making for pleasure; and nobody could deny that he was doing the mistress of the farm real knight-service by this voluntary contribution of his labour at a busy time.'

In *The Romantic Adventures of a Milkmaid* Baron von Xanten sees the hay-makers in the water-meadows. 'The white shirt-sleeves of the mowers glistened in the sun, the scythes flashed, voices echoed, snatches of song floated about, and there were glimpses of red waggon-wheels, purple gowns, and many-coloured handkerchiefs.' After the grass was cut it was left to dry out, turned, and made into small heaps or haycocks for further drying. Suke Damson and Fitzpiers romp in a field of half-made hay in *The Woodlanders*: hayfields were always attractive, with their heaps of sweet-smelling herbage. When it was dry the hay was made into a rick, either in the farmyard, or in a field where it would later be needed for the stock. Hay ricks needed careful building and management before balers were introduced in the twentieth century, because ricked hay continues to heat and thereby cure. If there is too much moisture, it can overheat and burst into flames, leaving just a remarkably small heap of ashes. Even with modern machinery good haymaking is a delicate procedure, dominated by the weather.

*Another photograph of the hurdle-maker.*

*Top Left:*
*Part of Woodbury Hill fair in the 1890s. The sheep 'were penned before the morning had far advanced, the dog belonging to each flock being tied to the corner of the pen containing it. Alleys for pedestrians intersected the pens, which soon became crowded with buyers and sellers'* Far from the Madding Crowd.

The sheep needed quantities of hurdles to keep them penned in on the arable, and cribs to feed the ewes and lambs from. These were supplied by the coppicing industry, seen along with other woodland crafts in *The Woodlanders*. The village of Little Hintock (a composite of several real villages in north Dorset) earned its living from the woodlands that surround it. Melbury, 'the timber, bark, and copse-ware merchant', markets the produce of the timber-fellers, turners, bark-strippers and hurdle-makers he employs. He rents copses and buys timber from the land-owner, which was the usual arrangement for cropping woodlands, and one which meant that men without capital could start in the business. When Giles Winterborne loses his house he buys 'several acres of brushwood standing', having received a large order for hurdles and other copseware. He and his men cut the young hazel, which has been left to grow for five to seven years, taking the poles to make hurdles and cribs, and the smaller stuff (or brushwood) for pea sticks, and for firing ovens. Everything had a use: even the chippings and refuse from hurdle making were used on the workmen's fires.

Melbury buys not only hazel coppice, but also large trees, and he has a saw pit to convert these to planks. Before the introduction of

*The saw pit* (foreground) *belonging to Mr Rapsey of Wootton Fitzpaine in West Dorset. He was a joiner as well as timber merchant. The tree trunk is in position to begin sawing, when the top sawyer would stand on the tree and the bottom sawyer go down the steps in the pit below. Long narrow coarse saws were used to reduce the tree to planks, which were then stored for at least two years to season them before use.*

*In the timber yard at Puddletown in 1894. Melbury's yard in* The Woodlanders *must have looked like this, filled with trees waiting to be sawn. The two men's clothes are remarkably similar, except that one wears dark shades, the other pale.*

machinery it was easier to put the bottom sawyer into a pit than to raise the trunk of a tree. The poor bottom dog or sawyer got showered in sawdust, but the top dog had the difficult job of guiding the saw along the right line. A wheelwright from Dorset recalled his apprenticeship, when all planks were still cut by hand, and it was possible to select the curved pieces of wood needed to make the wagons while they were still part of the tree. When machine sawing came in this was no longer done, and wagons became straighter and more box-like. In *The Woodlanders* the wagons are still 'built on those ancient lines whose proportions

Pulling tree trunks onto a pole carriage in Dorset in the 1880s or 1890s. The right hand horse is waiting to help pull the pole carriage when loaded. The other one is pulling another tree trunk onto the pole carriage with a chain.

have been ousted by modern patterns, their shapes bulging and curving at the base and ends like Trafalgar line-of-battle ships, with which venerable hulks, indeed, these vehicles evidenced a constructive spirit curiously in harmony.'

Oak was often grown for timber in the coppices, and when felled the bark was stripped off to be used for tanning. Marty South joins the workmen for this, all of them using a tool made from 'a horse's legbone fitted into a handle and filed to an edge,' to detach the bark from the tree.

The hero, Giles Winterborne, 'had a marvellous power of making trees grow. Although he would seem to shovel in the earth quite carelessly there was a sort of sympathy between himself and the fir, oak, or beech that he was operating on; so that the roots took hold of the soil in a few days.' 'He put most of the roots towards the south-west; for, he said, in forty years' time, when some great gale is blowing from that quarter, the trees will require the strongest holdfast on that side to stand against it and not fall.' In the autumn he travelled with his cider press. Grace sees him 'as the fruit-god and the wood-god in alternation: sometimes leafy and smeared with green lichen, as she had seen him amongst the sappy boughs of the plantations: sometimes cider-stained and starred with

178

*Children gathering furze at Stanton St. Gabriel on the west Dorset coast in the 1890s. Clym Yeobright becomes a professional furze cutter in* The Return of the Native, *cutting gorse and binding it with brambles to make faggots. These were the best fuel for bread ovens, producing a fast flash heat. Many ancient farms had furze-plots close to them, and rights to cut furze on common land appear in many old leases.*

apple-pips, as she had met him on his return from cider-making . . . with his vats and presses beside him.' He was at one with the woods and trees.

*Left:*

*Isaac Riglar, spar maker of Tolpuddle, in the 1880s. The straps around his knees were called yorkers; his thighs are protected by pads of leather. In* The Woodlanders *Marty South makes spars (right), the quartered hazel sticks used to fix the straw or reed down when thatching. 'To produce them she took up each gad [hazel rod left], looked critically at it from end to end, cut it to length, split it into four, and sharpened each of the quarters with dexterous blows, which brought it to a triangular point.' In a day and half the night she makes a thousand and a half spars, earning two shillings and threepence.*

Bockhampton is on the most westerly tongue of a huge area of heathland that, before reclamation, stretched through Dorset east to Bournemouth and then by way of the New Forest all the way to Southampton. It was cut by wide fertile river valleys, which contrasted with the bleak and unproductive heath. In about 1750 one-sixth of Dorset (100,000 acres) was heathland, but this had dropped to 75,000 acres in 1811, and by 1896 there were only 56,000 acres left. The extent today (14,000 acres) is only about one-sixth that of 1750. The rest has been reclaimed for agriculture, planted with conifers, or built over. For example Bournemouth was built on heathland from the 1840s.

179

*Warmwell Heath in May 1912. 'As with some persons who have long lived apart, solitude seemed to look out of its countenance. It had a lonely face, suggesting tragical possibilities'* The Return of the Native.

At this same period, that of *The Return of the Native*, the heath was being cleared elsewhere. Wildeve's Patch has been 'after long and laborious years brought into cultivation. The man who had discovered that it could be tilled died of the labour: the man who succeeded him in possession ruined himself in fertilizing it. Wildeve came . . . and received the honours due to those who had gone before.'

The heathland is central to *The Return of the Native*, which opens with a description of the heath at twilight, when 'the sombre

180

*Puddletown Heath in 1898. The tracks are so poor that two horses are needed even for a smallish cart.*

*The James family, photographed by Lea when they were at Puddletown in 1899. Lea's original caption says that the family lived a nomadic life, but were not of gypsy extraction. There seem to be six children living in the caravan and crude tent with their parents. In the foreground there are bunches of primroses in a bowl, which they probably gathered and sold.*

*The daughter standing on boards in the river is perhaps filling a bucket attached to the end of the rope. Sitting under the hedge they are making pegs: peeled hazel sticks can be seen to the right of Mr James, and he is surrounded by shavings.*

stretch of rounds and hollows seemed to rise and meet the evening gloom in pure sympathy, the heath exhaling darkness as rapidly as the heavens precipitated it . . . when other things sank brooding to sleep the heath appeared to awake and listen.' The novel sees the heath through its full yearly cycle, celebrating its strangeness 'like man, slighted and enduring; and withal singularly colossal and mysterious in its swarthy monotony'. A pond on the heath is the setting for several of Hardy's poems: this, from 'Neutral Tones', may be Rushy Pond, near his birthplace.

> We stood by the pond that winter day.
> And the sun was white, as though chidden of God.
> And a few leaves lay on the starving sod;
> – They had fallen from an ash, and were gray.

In March 'the heath showed its first faint signs of awakening from the winter trance . . . A timid animal world had come to life for the season.' Toads, tadpoles and newts were to be seen in the ponds. It is the beginning of summer before the 'moist hollows of the heath' are fully green with ferns, and its glory is seen not in spring, but when 'the July sun shone over Egdon and fired its crimson heather scarlet. It was the one season of the year . . . in which the heath was gorgeous . . . it followed the green or young-fern period, and preceded the brown period, when the heath-bells and ferns would wear the russet tinges . . . to be in turn displaced by the dark hue of the winter period.'

*Part of Egdon Heath. In the early nineteenth century there were wild ponies on the Dorset heaths, called heathcroppers, as there are still in the New Forest. In the early morning and evening it is even now possible to see deer, especially on the margins of the Dorset woods and heaths.*

Egdon was Hardy's name for the heaths running east from Dorchester to Poole, after the huge Iron Age hillfort of Eggardon in western Dorset. In fact there is no general name and it appears on maps with the name of the nearest village appended – Winfrith Heath, Puddletown Heath and so on.

When Hardy was re-reading his novels in proof for the Wessex edition of 1912 he wrote to a friend saying that Clym Yeobright, in *The Return of the Native* 'is the nicest of all my heroes and *not a bit like me*'. Clym loved the heath; 'he was permeated with its scenes, with its substance and with its odours. He might be said to be its product. His eyes had first opened thereon; with its appearance all the first images of his memory were mingled; his estimate of life had been coloured by it.' This was true of Hardy himself, since his birthplace was on the edge of the heath, as recorded in his first poem to survive, 'Domicilium', written before he was twenty-one.

> Behind the scene is wilder. Heath and furze
> Are everything that seems to grow and thrive
> Upon the uneven ground. A stunted thorn
> Stands here and there, indeed . . .

Hardy told Herman Lea of 'the childish fears he had felt crossing that lonely stretch of heathland by himself when it was dusk, or

*Pig-killing outside the pigsties in the 1890s. The pigs are dead – they have been hung up by the rope in the doorway, stunned and then bled to death. On the left a pig is being scalded, and on the right one that has been scalded is being scraped to remove its bristles. The man in the centre is sharpening his knife ready to start jointing the pigs. The joints will be soaked in brine and then smoked to produce bacon.*

even at times quite dark, and the particular, indefinable fear that gripped him when the whole sombre surroundings were shrouded in dense fog.'

The heathland and the heathfolk are pagan to Hardy, timeless and unchanging. 'The impulses of all such outlandish hamlets are pagan still: in these spots homage to nature, self-adoration, frantic gaieties, fragments of Teutonic rites to divinities whose names are forgotten, seem in some way to have survived mediaeval doctrine'; that is, Christianity.

Hardy thought that 'the untameable . . . thing that Egdon now was it always had been. Civilization was its enemy; and ever since the beginning of vegetation its soil had worn the same antique brown dress.' He would have been surprised to know that modern research has shown that the Dorset heathlands were created in the Bronze Age, nearly 4,000 years ago. Analysis of the pollen preserved in the heathland shows that it was originally rather poor woodland, and that prehistoric clearance for agriculture destroyed the natural balance of soil and vegetation, making the

*Poultry feeding in the 1890s. Many smallholders and farmers' wives kept poultry. This looks a very mixed lot, with big brown chicken, white chicken and geese. The wood in the stack has no bark on: it was probably stripped for sale. Oak bark was used in the tanning process.*

original poor soils even more unproductive. After the prehistoric clearance, grazing, turf- and furze-cutting, and fires, all prevented the regeneration of trees. Civilisation was not in fact its enemy at all; it created it, and maintained it.

Life in this rural nineteenth century world, especially the farming run willy-nilly on 'organic' lines, with its crops produced without spraying, its wide hedges, woods, and ponds, has not only a nostalgic appeal. The farm then co-existed with wildlife, and the range and quantity of wild flowers, trees, birds and animals in the countryside pleased all those, like Hardy, who observed them. The careful rotation of crops and application of farmyard manure kept the land in good heart. There was no need to employ chemical fertilizers whose side-effects are not understood. This, and the use of many resources we now waste, such as straw split and woven for hats and so forth, hazel coppiced for hurdles, pegs, and fuel, or even dandelion roots ground and fed to horses as a tonic, appeal to all who see our own age as spendthrift. The rural industries seem attractively primitive, their products charmingly simple, and the craftsmen enviable for their satisfying lives.

185

In fact we create an arcadian dream of a simpler, better, rather static world, where somehow everyone was both more practical and more fulfilled. There is even an odd platonic attraction, in the face of our own restless and rootless mobility, to the idea of everyone knowing their station, and trying to fill it.

But this dream is just that. There is nothing arcadian and fulfilling in not knowing how you are to feed your children on an agricultural labourer's wage; in having to live in a tied cottage when the only alternative is a town slum; in working twelve hours a day (more at busy times), with no hope of retiring finally except to the workhouse or to the sufferance of your poverty-stricken family. The farming that produced these beautiful landscapes was bedded on the terrible wages of labourers. Certainly you may have beautifully laid hedges if you are paying the man laying them only ten shillings a week. If you must pay him a living wage, it is a very different story.

Even the idea of society as static is an illusion; it has probably never been so. Hardy writes of families who go up and down the social scale, and in the nineteenth century it was even possible to buy your way into the aristocracy. At the other end of the scale 'modern' jobs such as those on the railways, in the towns, in the police, and most importantly for women, in teaching, were completely altering the outlook and prospects for the labouring classes. Even before agricultural labourers took to changing their jobs frequently, families were not rooted in one place for ever: they travelled in search of work, or to be servants – like Hardy's mother, who went into service at Maiden Newton in central Dorset. Many went further. When times were hard a considerable number left the country altogether, hoping to find a better life in America, Canada or Australia.

Neither farmers nor labourers enjoyed the wild flora and fauna: except with the woods and pasture, they spent most of their lives fighting them. The bright blue flowers of the corn-cockle look lovely in a cornfield, but their seeds are poisonous, and have to be carefully removed from the grain. Farmers fought weeds with every means then in their power; the only reason sprays were not used was that they were yet to be invented. Rabbits would eat all the corn growing on the margins of the fields, and small boys stood all day to scare the birds from germinating seeds. Many farmers cherished their prime stock, but when the animals were less valuable, there was more cruelty. Hardy brought a private case against two men who beat a cow they were driving along in front of his house; and such incidents were common.

Of course most people are much better off now, but the countryside has suffered. There must be a middle way between the human exploitation of the nineteenth century and the nature exploitation of our own, which increasingly threatens to leave us with nothing but monotonous green deserts between our cities.

Hardy had a slightly romantic idea of farming; he was never a farmer or a labourer, but he had a deep and informed sympathy with the plight of the workers on the land, putting human necessity above picturesqueness. He would surely rejoice at the improved condition of country people today, but curse our destruction of his countryside.

Thomas Hardy's fiction of course contains far more than the description of rural life and its ways, yet such settings are

187

all-important in his work. They form its deep background, its most remembered décor, much of its characteristic key. The photographs here are of its visual reality, and so must ignore all the transmutations that Hardy's literary genius effected on that mere physical or literal outward form. The world shown here is without his magic, but as he himself would have first seen and known it — very much his raw material. This seemingly became increasingly rich to him as he aged. He lost all interest in travelling in his last years, saying that there was more than he could ever know or understand within a mile of Max Gate. In his seventies he published 'Afterwards':

When the Present has latched its postern behind my
tremulous stay
And the May month flaps its golden green leaves like
wings,
Delicate-filmed as new-spun silk, will the neighbours say,
"He was a man who used to notice such things"?

If it be in the dusk when, like an eyelid's soundless blink,
The dew-fall hawk comes crossing the shades to alight
Upon the wind-warped upland thorn, a gazer may think,
"To him this must have been a familiar sight"

# Index Italicised page numbers indicate an illustration

# Thomas Hardy, his Life and Works

**1840** Born on June 2nd at Upper Bockhampton, eldest child of Thomas and Jemina Hardy.

**1856** Articled to John Hicks, architect of Dorchester.

**1862** Moves to London.

**1867** Returns to Dorset.

**1868 −89** Writes *The Poor Man and the Lady*, which is rejected by publishers.

**1871** *Desperate Remedies* published.

**1872** *Under the Greenwood Tree* published.

**1873** *A Pair of Blue Eyes* published.

**1874** Marries Emma Gifford, and *Far from the Madding Crowd* published.

**1875** Moves from London to Swanage.

**1876** Living in Yeovil and then Sturminster Newton: *The Hand of Ethelberta* published.

**1878** Moves to Tooting, and *The Return of the Native* published.

**1880** *The Trumpet Major* published.

**1881** Moves to Wimborne, Dorset, and *A Laodicean* published.

**1882** *Two on a Tower* published.

**1883** Moves back to Dorchester.

**1885** Moves into Max Gate.

**1886** *The Mayor of Casterbridge* published.

**1887** *The Woodlanders* published.

**1888** *Wessex Tales* (short stories) published.

**1891** *A Group Of Noble Dames* (short stories) and *Tess of the D'Urbervilles* published.

**1894** *Life's Little Ironies* (short stories) published.

**1895** *Jude the Obscure* published.

**1897** *The Well-beloved* published.

**1898** *Wessex Poems*, his first volume of poetry, published.

**1901** *Poems of the Past and Present* published.

**1904 −08** *The Dynasts*, an epic drama, published in three parts.

**1909** *Time's Laughingstocks* (poetry) published.

**1912** Emma Hardy dies.

**1913** *A Changed Man and other Tales* published. Hermann Lea's *Thomas Hardy's Wessex* published.

**1914** Marries Florence Dugdale, and *Satires of Circumstance* (poetry) published.

**1917** *Moments of Vision* (poetry) published.

**1922** *Late Lyrics and Earlier* (poetry) published.

**1923** *The Famous Tragedy of the Queen of Cornwall* published.

**1925** *Human Shows, Far Phantasies, Songs, and Trifles* (poetry) published.

**1928** Dies at Max Gate on January 11th, aged 87, and his last volume of poetry – *Winter Words* – published in October.